M000104041

Doc Hensley's enthusiasm, energy, and encyclopedia of ideas are captured here in print. If you've always wanted to do something with your writing, here's how to get going.

**Liz Curtis Higgs**
**Author,** *Bad Girls of the Bible*

There are no shortcuts to writing well and getting published. But there is a Ferrari that will get you down the road a whole lot faster. This book is it! Strap yourself in and pull away from the pack. Doc Hensley has done it all in the world of writing—and now he's giving it all away in this one super-charged volume. Doc helped me cross the finish line with my book—and he can do the same for you!

**Jon Gauger, Moody Radio Host**
**Author,** *If I Could Do It All Over Again*

Doc Hensley is my favorite writing teacher, hands down. I've never hosted a writers conference without asking him to speak—and when parents ask where to send their budding writers to college, I tell 'em Taylor University, Upland, Indiana, where they'll learn more their first month under Doc Hensley than in four years anywhere else. Now Doc has compiled an exhaustive compendium of advice based on a lifetime of teaching…and doing. Make *Finding Success with Your Dream Writing Projects* your go-to guide to all things writing, and you can't go wrong."

**Jerry B. Jenkins**
**Author of 21** *New York Times* **best-sellers,**
**including** *Left Behind,* **and owner of**
**The Jerry Jenkins Writers Guild**

No one, and I mean no one, is better at teaching writing than Dennis E. Hensley. Open this book and learn from the master.

**Bill Myers**
**Author,** *Eli* **and** *McGee & Me*

I've known Dennis Hensley for the past twenty-plus years, have read his books, listened to him deliver keynote talks, worked with him on projects, and taught with him at Taylor University. He is truly one of the best authors and speakers on writing with his practical and professional presentations.

**James Watkins**
**Recipient, Campus Life Book of the Year Award**

There is no one better than Dr. Dennis E. Hensley at equipping, inspiring, and educating writers to fulfill their dreams. Only the inventor of the alphabet has done more for writers and writing."

**Bob Hostetler**
**Author, *The Bard and the Bible***

This highly creative guide is delightful to read—and should be referred to again and again by anyone serious about the craft of writing. How I wish I could have had it when I was teaching college students! The steps to creating fiction and nonfiction that will catch an editor's attention are well illustrated with innovative ideas. Both beginning and advanced writers will find the guidance they need in order to become published.

**Marjorie Sell Stewart, MA**
**Retired English professor, Northwest University,**
**Kirkland WA**

I felt like I was in the classroom with Doc Hensley as he revealed secrets of not only his success, but those of his myriad students. Everything you need to learn about mastering the art of writing, speaking, and believing in your delivery of both is captured within these pages.

**Joyce Oglesby**
**Host of the *Just Ask Joyce*® Show,**
**WFIA-FM, Louisville**

My long-time friend Dennis E. Hensley is both a teacher and an entertainer. He makes learning how to write a joyous experience. When people ask me how to become a novelist or screenwriter, I tell them to spend time reading the writings of Doc Hensley.

**Ken Wales**
**Executive producer, *Amazing Grace* and *Christy***

# Finding Success with Your Dream Writing Projects

# Finding Success with Your Dream Writing Projects

Dennis E. Hensley

*with*
Diana Savage

Bold Vision Books
PO Box 2011
Friendswood, Texas 77549

Copyright © Dennis E. Hensley 2017


ISBN 9780997851489
LCCN 2017932232


Cover by Amy Allen
Cover Photo © Mikhail Dudarev | Dreamstime.com
Interior design by ƙae Creative Solutions

Published in the United States of America.

Published in Association with MacGregor Literary Agency,
Manzanita, OR 97130



Bold Vision Books
PO Box 2011
Friendswood, Texas 77549

# Dedication

This book is dedicated to my granddaughter Grace, who has a marvelous imagination and a natural bent toward writing. She brings me joy.

Dennis E. Hensley

# Table of Contents

## Chapter 5 – The Nitty-Gritty of Fiction~94

Writing Micro Fiction
The Parameters of Violence in Fiction
Suspending Disbelief
Once Before a Time: Creating Prequels
Keep Readers Hooked Through Subplots
How to Write Series Novels: Linking Past to Present

## Chapter 6 – Spot-On Dialogue, Characters, and Settings~114

Ask All the Wrong Questions
The Fascination of Physically Challenged Characters
When to Make Fictional Characters Versions of You—And
    When Not To
Talking the Talk: Exercises to Master Dialogue
Make Your Dialogue Sparkle
How to Nail Your Fiction Settings

## Chapter 7 – Develop a Support Team~133

My Biggest Mistake as a Beginning Writer
Grow with a Mentor
Your Critique Partners
Offering the Blemished Lamb: Why Editing Is Crucial
Learning from a Master Editor
The Top Ten Bad Moves for Freelance Writers
Ghostwriting Isn't Spooky
Create a Database of Experts

## Chapter 8 – Time, Money, and the Freelance Writer~158

Make the Most of Your Writing Time
Maximize Your Book-Writing Energies
Recognize the Three Pitfalls of Literary Citizenship
Take the Free Out of Freelance Writing
How to Negotiate for Better Payments

# Acknowledgments

I wish to thank my wife Rose for decades of love and encouragement.

Certain writer friends of mine have had a positive impact on my life and career, most notably Jerry B. Jenkins, Bob Hostetler, Lin Johnson, Diana E. Savage, Jim Watkins, Linda Taylor, George and Karen Porter, Rachael Phillips, Reg Forder, Bill Myers, John Ingrisano, and Bill and Liz Curtis Higgs.

I owe much gratitude to my agent, Jerry "Chip" MacGregor, for advice, friendship, and writing insights.

Thank you, one and all.


Dennis E. Hensley

# Introduction

**For two decades** I have been director of the Department of Professional Writing at Taylor University. Of the more than sixty books I've written, eight have been texts on subjects related to grammar, punctuation, spelling, style, format, technique, plotting, narrative drive, dialogue, character development, and creative brainstorming. I was a regional correspondent for more than twenty years for *Writer's Digest* and a contributing editor and columnist for *Writer's Journal, Writer's World, Christian Communicator,* and *Advanced Christian Writer.*

All this teaching and writing has provided mountains of material to convert into blog posts for my website, dochensley.com. One day my webmaster, Diana Savage, observed, "We could compile these columns and articles into a compendium for writers. After all, you've spent a lifetime studying professional writing, and people need to have ready access to your hard-won insights."

That sounded good to me, so I gave her the green light. Like a puzzle solver, Diana arranged all the various columns and posts into categories and turned them into a book manuscript. Within its context, you'll find advice and real-life anecdotes on how to get started as a professional writer. You'll find tips on enhancing writing technique, insights on how to cope with rejection, innovative ideas for jump-starting your creativity, ways to overcome specific fiction challenges, suggestions for developing a support team, methods of managing your time and money as a freelancer, and concepts for promoting your work. It's a rousing roundup of systems to enhance your success as a writer.

Educational books are no longer static sources of information. Just as this text was born of a series of blog posts and online lessons, it now provides an entrance for you to continue your education by linking with webinars, chat rooms, and websites that provide contemporary insights, industry updates, and expanding venues.

This book is your foundation. Read it. Practice its methods. Follow its advice. Review its chapters often. But then go online to explore, expand, and enhance your writing endeavors. You can't lose. While drawing on the years of experience behind this book, you'll also be accessing all emerging developments in publishing.

What a great time to be a writer!

# Chapter 1
# Off to a Great Start

**Great Start Tip 1**
**Start, Then Gloat**

**When I attended** my forty-fifth high school class reunion, someone brought a copy of the senior-year edition of our school literary magazine. I had two short pieces in that issue. When I reread them decades later as the author of more than fifty books, I cringed at how pathetic both items seemed. They were comedy pieces (supposedly), but they were lightweight, silly, and stilted. I was embarrassed—until I flipped through the rest of the magazine and discovered that, as bad as my writing had been, it was far better than anything the other students had written. Yeah, my stuff was bad, but theirs was horrendous.

This has led me to two good lessons to pass along. First, as a new writer, *start*. Start poorly, perhaps, but start. You can only get better. Second, gloat. Maybe you aren't writing for *The New Yorker*, but you are in print. That puts you a step ahead of the thousands of hacks who are getting only rejection letters.

You may be wondering if I'm speaking tongue-in-cheek. I'm not. I run the professional writing department at a private college. Each year I accept thirty-five new first-year students who have the goal of one day making a full-time living strictly from writing and editing. They arrive with ambition, energy, and passion, and they are better writers than most other eighteen-year-olds nationwide. But then the roof caves in on them.

When they get their first assignments back from me, they are stunned. Some (and here, I'm serious) cry. They've never seen so much red ink in all their lives.

The problem is, they've been "good" writers since fifth grade, always earning A's, but they are a long way from being *professional* writers. They know grammar, but they can't write a grabber lead to save their lives. They know spelling, but the dialogue they create would embarrass a marionette. They know type fonts and formatting and texting, but they have no clue how to handle foreshadowing, flashbacks, or elements of irony.

So, they start poorly. But the point is, they start. They develop a turtle-shell hide that enables them to see criticism and editing by me and by other professional writers as the code-breaking of the secret to getting published. After four years of researching, writing, revising, and marketing, they reach the gloating stage. They walk out of college with a degree, a large portfolio of published manuscripts, and a series of job offers from publishers, editors, and agents. That is to say, about 70 percent of them.

Along the way, about three out of every ten students who enter my program drop out. They lose the vision they came in with, or they are too vain to realize they aren't as good as they thought they were as writers, or they run out of energy and drive, or they get steamrolled by the other students who begin to excel at getting published.

## Stay the Course

Writing isn't easy. Making a living as a writer is a lot harder than most people realize. But, as I tell my students, "A bad day as a writer is better than a good day as a fast-food worker." A waiter or waitress may occasionally get a nice tip, but he or she won't change lives or captivate minds or alter the course of history. Writers, however, are in the business of all three of these miracles.

18

So, where does this leave you? Maybe you've looked at what you've written thus far, and you haven't been impressed. Join the club. After his first book was published, W. Somerset Maugham literally burned every draft of his failed novels and rejected short stories. He was terrified someone would one day discover what a poor writer he had been. How silly. Why smash your Little League trophies just because you've signed a Major League contract?

Give yourself more time. We all start poorly, but we don't have to stay that way. I plan to rewrite those two lame stories in my high school literary magazine. It's never too late to get better.

## Great Start Tip 2
## Be Wary of Artificial
## Intelligence

**Ahead of me** in line at the library, a middle-aged woman was watching a teenage girl blitzing text messages on her cell phone. It seemed as though the young girl's thumbs were gyrating at supersonic speed.

The older woman looked at me, nodded at the girl, and said, "These young people are technological wizards. Aren't they amazing?"

"Not in the least," I said. "In fact, most of them are quite vapid."

The woman looked confused. "But look at her—how fast she can read messages and transmit responses. She's communicating

19

at lightning speed, whereas I can barely remember how to download voicemail on my phone."

"Don't confuse manual dexterity with mental competence," I cautioned. "Sure, she can send truncated text messages to her friends, and she can do it rapidly. But what is she saying? Nothing. *Absolutely nothing.* Most of these kids can't spell correctly; they can't organize a paragraph, and they sure as heck can't create syntactical formations that make any impact on readers. They're just noisemakers."

"Noisemakers?"

"Indeed," I said. "If my four-year-old granddaughter comes to my house and pounds the piano keys up and down the scale, she's showing rapid movement and manual dexterity, but she's certainly not producing music. She's just making noise. Likewise, if a young person is pounding up and down on the keyboard of a cell phone, rifling text messages hither and yon, none of that is great literature or even quality letter-writing. It's just noise."

## Techno-druggies

In my work as a writers conference teacher, I've discovered in recent years that more and more novice writers are becoming very dependent on (yea, addicted to) technology to shore up their weaknesses as communicators. First came spell-check programs. After that came grammar-check programs. And now, according to recent news items, the next offering will be "style-check" software. At this rate, we may one day end up with robot ghostwriters. Gosh, folks, think of the passion produced by *those* apparatuses. It will give a whole new meaning to the term "klunker" novels.

I'm climbing on a soapbox about this because would-be professional writers need to understand that buying the latest iPad or Kindle or laptop computer is no panacea regarding publishing success. Writers need to master sentence structuring, plot formatting, character development, vocabulary enrichment, and setting enhancements. Until these skills are mastered, no quality writing will be produced. You can sit a child at a grand piano, but if all she can do is plunk out "Twinkle,

Twinkle, Little Star," the fact that her instrument is worth $25,000 will not make her a virtuoso. You can parallel this to the untrained writer who sits in front of the latest word processor that has been programmed with the most advanced software. It will still come down to garbage in, garbage out (or noise in, noise out, the metaphor of your choice).

## Seeking the Mentor

The question will arise, "But where do I get that training?" Today it's easier to respond to that question than ever before. In bygone eras, it was a common belief (desperate hope, more likely) that "when the student is ready, the teacher will appear." For the twenty-first century, I believe we should rephrase that as "when the student is ready, the teacher should be sought." Would-be writers should invest in themselves before they invest in expensive hardware. And here's how to make the right kind of investments.

1. **Marry up.** Join a writers club in your area that has writers who are better at the craft than you are. Listen to their lectures. Ask them to critique your manuscripts. Find out what books they're reading. Use these people to get introductions to editors and literary agents. Benefit from osmosis by associating with successful writers.

2. **Read voraciously, and take voluminous notes.** You can borrow books about writing from your public library. You can swap books about writing among friends and colleagues. You can read blogs written by editors and agents and professional writers. You can read writing trade journals at the library or, in many cases, as online periodicals. You'll be able to create notebooks or computer documents filled with transcriptions of your notes, which you then can review regularly.

3. **Go back to school.** Many community and regional college campuses have weekend and evening classes as part of their continuing education programs. For a modest fee, you can audit classes in literature, expository writing, advanced composition, poetry, fiction, or journalism. Many times these

courses are taught by newspaper reporters or freelance writers who enjoy picking up a little extra money by moonlighting as adjunct professors. They know their stuff.

4. **Log the time.** Whether you have a 1948 Underwood model (don't laugh—Woody Allen still does all of his writing on a manual typewriter) or a state-of-the-art laptop, you are still going to have to get better by trial and error. There is an old joke about a man walking down the street. He is lost, so he says to a stranger, "Excuse me, but how do I get to Carnegie Hall?" The stranger replies, "Practice, practice, practice." It's no different in the field of professional writing. If you want to be a writer, start writing.

**The Wish List**

Now, having said all this, I'll make a confession to you. I own an excellent laptop computer. I own an iPad. I own a smartphone. I'm certainly not against taking advantage of modern technology. However, the only true word processor is the human brain.

So, before I ever made any investments in techno-toys, I first invested in my training and education as a writer. I would recommend the same priority to you. Sure, you make a wish list of the gadgets you'd like to own one day. But prior to that, buy into the concept that you need to secure *real* intelligence before you secure *artificial* intelligence.

**Great Start Tip 3
Take Me Out of the
Bawl Game**

**I can see** direct parallels between the worlds of freelance writing and professional baseball. Even the catchphrases and lingo are the same.

When I was a young reporter for the *Muncie Star*, I would have to start each morning by "pitching" ideas to the city editor. He would respond, "No, you're out in left field on that idea" or "Stay with that one until you knock it out of the park" or "Sorry, you struck out on that one." If one of our regular reporters was off covering a court case and another story was breaking, the city editor would scream, "Hensley, you're on deck, so you go cover the police beat" or "Hensley, you pinch hit for Anderson over at city hall."

If a politician would suddenly announce she was entering the race for mayor, the city editor would say, "Whoa! She threw us a curve on that one." If I was having a hard time digging up facts for a story, the city editor would say, "You can do it, Slugger" or "I've got a hole on page one, Hensley, and you're batting cleanup. Bring it home, baby, bring it home." If I was at my house on my day off and the city editor had to call me in for some overtime, he'd say, "Get off the bench, Hensley, we've got a five-car pileup on the expressway, and I need you to cover it."

I could continue with endless examples, proving that baseball metaphors are always "at bat" amidst writers. However, one particular phrase dominates all others when it comes to baseball and freelance writing. It was said by Tom Hanks in the movie *A League of Their Own.* Say it with me, folks: "There's no crying in baseball!"

The same rule applies to writing. If one of your manuscripts gets rejected, you cannot cry. You have to rewrite it. If your elevator pitch gets blown off by an editor, you cannot cry. You have to go back and refine it. If your coauthor quits or dies in the middle of a project and you're left having to do all the remaining work, you cannot cry. You have to step up to the plate and finish the book. If your book finally gets published and the critics rip it to shreds, you cannot cry. You have to sit at the computer and write a better book the next time.

As writers, we all strike out now and then. We cannot cry when that happens. We can bunt, steal, walk, or switch hit. But, no, there's no bawling in the ballgame of writing.

### Great Start Tip 4
### Strategies for Expanding
### Your Horizons

**Whenever you're at** a writers conference, make it a point to attend sessions on topics you normally consider out of your interest range. If you are primarily a poet, attend a session on scriptwriting. If you usually write only short stories, attend a session on writing devotionals.

If you can't attend a conference—or even if you do—you can still follow some procedures that will help you discover new talents within yourself and new markets for your manuscripts. Here's how to go about it.

Begin by exposing yourself to a variety of magazines. Take your copy of *Writer's Market* and *Christian Writer's Market Guide* and turn to categories you've never sold material to before. If you are a mature person, spend time analyzing teen magazines. If you are Caucasian, then look up magazines aimed at ethnic readers. If you are from the Midwest, look up periodicals published for people of other regions of the country.

Having selected a new category of magazines to study, check online or write to each magazine and ask for its guidelines for writers and a sample copy of a back issue. Enclose a check for the cover price of the magazine as a courtesy if a backdated version is not available online. Later, study the magazine carefully. What sort of advertising does it carry? For example, if it has numerous ads for baby food and toys, this would be a great place for articles about child care. How progressive or conservative are its editorials and/or articles? You'll have to match that slant if you plan to please the editor.

Use a highlighting pen to help you analyze how long the articles are, how dialogue-heavy the copy is, what sorts of leads and transitions and endings the editor prefers, and whether or not there are any taboo areas (such as the use of slang or references to the "other" political party).

Study the writing style of the magazine. Some periodicals refer to women by last name only (Smith, Wilson), whereas others insist that a title appear before a woman's name (Mrs. Smith, Dr. Wilson).

Some periodicals like the author to use a light style with contractions, quotations, short paragraphs, and humor. Other periodicals prefer formal prose with paragraphs that contain the traditional topic sentences, support sentences, and transition sentences.

Study the format of the article. Does the editor like subheads, sidebars, reference notes, photos, charts, maps, diagrams, cartoons, or other supplemental materials to accompany the article? If so, you'll need to obtain them or write them.

Look at the table of contents. Is the magazine divided into sub-categories (cooking, crafts, child care, entertainment)? Does it use non-fiction *and* fiction? Does it feature an interview with anyone? (If so, is it in a question-and-answer format or more of a feature format?) Does it use travel articles, book reviews, or guest editorials? Look for any place you might break in.

After you have studied the guidelines and analyzed the sample magazine for format and style, compare it with other magazines in the same category. What topics seem to recur in all the magazines? These will be the "hot" topics. What sorts of experts do these magazines seek out for advice? These will be the kinds of people you, too, will need to locate and interview.

Fortified by your new knowledge of this area of writing, prepare a couple of query letters and send them to the editors. Whenever you land an assignment, complete it well. When that article is published, use a copy of it as a way of introducing yourself to editors of other similar magazines. Keep working this same plan until you've cracked them all. Then keep writing for them, but move on to another completely new category of magazines. Keep expanding your knowledge and talents.

# Great Start Tip 5
# Use Stories to Help
# Readers Relate

**I was at** a social gathering one summer when I overheard a professor from a community college complaining about his math students. It seems they were having a hard time comprehending the behavioral characteristics of basic physics problems. For example, in trying to explain to them about growth or decay aspects of nuclear material, the prof found they could not comprehend "doubling initiative" or "half-life."

I told him I could see in an instant what his "problem" was (that's shoptalk for mathematicians, even though, personally, I still do addition by counting on my fingers and toes). I explained, "You haven't got a storyline they can relate to."

He looked totally baffled. "Storyline? We're talking about a mathematical equation."

"True enough," I agreed, "but for these students—and here I draw upon a technical term from your academic discipline—it just 'doesn't add up.' You're not explaining it in a way they can relate to it."

"Relate to it?" he echoed me again, making us sound like a bad ventriloquism act. "I'm not trying to make math touchy-feely. I just want the students to be able to grasp a concept so they can apply a process."

"Then hit them where they live," I said. "Don't tell them that the nuclear component degrades to a half-life after $X$ number of hours when impacted by $Y$ and $Z$. Who cares? Instead, tell them that drugs wash out of the bloodstream at different rates. For instance, after one full day, 25 percent of a dosage of Prozac will be dissipated, but 75 percent will still be in the system. So, give them a problem that begins with 100 mg of Prozac, and ask them to figure out how long the kidneys will have to work in order to decay the level of Prozac to below 10 mg. Basically, ask them to figure out what is the half-life of Prozac in the blood."

"And why would *that* be more interesting to them?" he asked.

"Because," I said, "when they go to get summer jobs, there is a big sign at the entrance of Lowe's, McDonald's, and Sears that says, 'Don't bother to apply for a job here if you can't pass the drug test.'"

## Helping Readers Relate

The basic flaw I find in nonfiction writing done by beginners is that the writers assemble a multitude of statistics, research, quotes, charts, and even timelines, but they leave the reader asking, "Yeah, but what's it got to do with me?" If readers are not shown how factual information will enhance their lives, they will have no use for it. No matter how accurate facts may be, they will be as boring as abstract physics problems if readers don't find anything there of takeaway value.

The way to guarantee that you deliver the goods is to pre-think your research. What do your readers *want* to know about the subject you're writing about? If you aren't sure, do some interviewing. Ask potential readers about their concerns, aspects of confusion, worries, hopes, and personal questions about the topic. Take a lot of notes. Target your material to respond to these questions.

Next, create stories that will draw readers into the explanation of your topic by relating it to something they are already familiar with or by introducing something they would enjoy investigating. For instance, let's say our friend the math prof wants to write about how to chart the influences of outside factors on the alteration of a geographic surface of a desert or a polar ice cap. (Yawn.) Normally, this would involve correlating coefficients of wind speed, sun rotation, and gravity pull. (My eyes are already drooping.)

However, let's turn it into a crime drama. A body has been found in the kitchen of a Chicago apartment on July 17 at 4:00 p.m. When discovered, the body temperature was 77.2 degrees Fahrenheit, and the kitchen's temperature was 70 degrees. If we can assume that John Smith's body temperature was a routine 98.6 F at the time of death, at what time was he murdered?

To solve this problem accurately, the students would have to understand how to prepare charts. They'd chart the routine temperatures of Chicago in mid-July. They'd chart how many degrees per hour a dead body cools when in a room of 70 F. They'd chart the ways the victim's height, weight, and cause of death (strangulation? blunt trauma?) factor into the equation.

Most people don't give a rip about the icy surfaces of the North Pole, but they get excited about learning how inner-city crimes can be solved...especially if they live in the inner city. Again I say, hit people where they live, and you'll hold their interest.

## The Drawstring

Once you've discovered what people want to learn about a topic, and once you've discovered how to give that information to them in a way that will hold their attention and/or sell them on the idea that it will be of direct use to them, you still need a finale.

In effect, you will need to pull everything together with a drawstring line that summarizes the lesson, underscores the moral, or spotlights the discovery.

Drawstring lines often begin with such summary expressions as, "This same process can be used for..." or "Thus, a comparable application of this system would be..." Most readers will already be aware of how the information they've just been taught or exposed to will provide takeaway value for them, but adding a drawstring line ensures that readers will see the *full* benefits of what has just been shared. It's like a bonus.

So, in sum (whoa...that math guy's had more of an impact on me than I realized), divide your research questions into segments, multiply your story illustrations, subtract any tedious research jargon, and your article will add up just fine.

# Chapter 2
# Tips for Terrific Technique

## Terrific Technique Tip 1
## Heed the Book Doctor—Give Your Novel a Face-Lift

**I encounter a** lot of people who have finished writing a novel but are having no success at selling it to a publisher. After a dozen or more rejections, they'll turn to a person like me—aka a "book doctor"—and ask, "So, what's wrong with my book?" Often, the answer is simple. These people have not learned that "all writing is rewriting." They've written a novel, but, as yet, they have not rewritten a novel.

If this is your situation, let me offer some guidance in how to give your novel the polish it needs to shine professionally.

1. **Get Outside Perspectives.** You know what the book is supposed to say, but to determine if it is saying it, you need outside readers. Find someone in your writers group to read it and give you specific feedback regarding narrative drive, character development, setting, dialogue, and theme. Likewise, consider hiring a high school or college English teacher to copyedit the pages and check grammar, syntax, punctuation, format, spelling, and transitions. This will reveal tangible aspects of the book that can be improved upon.

2. **Evaluate from Macro to Micro Elements.** Read your entire book, but chart it as you go along. How quickly does the lead hook the reader? Does the subplot become evident no later than chapter three? Where are the arcs of conflict, the surprises, the clever plot twists? Is the ultimate climactic scene dramatic enough? Does the denouement tie up all loose ends, answer all questions, and imply what the next phase of the characters' lives will be? By putting the whole book in your head (macro) while critiquing the individual elements (micro), you'll be inserting correct pieces that will eventually reveal the finished puzzle.

3. **Examine the Pattern and Flow of the Story.** Just because something is perfect in writing mechanics doesn't mean it is interesting. Consider key structural elements. Is the novel well-paced, motivating the reader to keep turning pages, or are there scenes that drag, passages of dialogue that are cluttered, and setups that have too much description and backstory? Are the flashbacks simply thrown in at random like narrative sludge, or do they seem a natural foundation for the overall story structure? Is there a consistency in the length of chapters, or are they a hodgepodge of plotting whims? These are all specific areas that publishers will judge harshly, so work to make them smooth.

4. **Scrutinize the Individual Words.** If you depend upon *ly* adverbs to assist your verbs (talked *quickly*, sang *merrily*), remove them, and insert stronger verbs that can stand alone (trilled, barked, rapped, prattled). Similarly, if you have a tendency to use too many *ing* verbs ("She was hurrying to get to work"), replace them with stronger verbs ("She raced to her job"). Weed out dull, indistinct verbs, too. Instead of saying, "She was outside the principal's office," say, "She paraded… She paced…She strode…She stood…She fumed outside the principal's office." Add verbal energy.

5. **Show, Don't Tell.** It's been drilled into you since childhood that actions speak louder than words. In fiction, this is especially true. For example, don't have a high-school girl tell

her arch rival, "You're not supposed to smoke in the bathroom. If you light up, I'm going to tell the teachers." Instead, write, "As Jennifer opened her purse and took out a cigarette and a lighter, Tina reached for the fire alarm."

What could have been a cliché has now become a page-turning face-off confrontation. That's what you want. Don't lull the reader to sleep with a rehash of what happened. Put him or her into the scene ready to witness the unfolding events.

I always compliment people who have shown the discipline it takes to actually write a novel. Most people have an idea for a story but not the professionalism to put it on paper. However, once that first draft has been purged from the mind, it is time to go back and fine-tune it. There is no shame in not producing a masterpiece on the first go-through. The shame is in letting it lose the beauty contest because you wouldn't give it the needed face-lift.

**Terrific Technique Tip 2
Add Zest with
Rhythm and Cadence**

**You can learn** a lot about holding people's attention if you listen to the spiel of a carnival barker. Notice the use of cadence and repetition in his pitch.

"Hurry, hurry, hurry. Come one, come all. Witness a true wonder of the world. Hurry, hurry, hurry. Step right up and see Joe-

Joe the Dog-Face Boy. He walks, he talks, he crawls on his belly like a reptile. Don't miss this amazing creature. Hurry, hurry, hurry!"

The repeated chant of "Hurry, hurry, hurry" gives a momentum to the come-on. It keeps drawing the listeners back to the point where something is in motion, something special is happening, something wonderful is occurring, and the audience needs to become part of it.

Nonfiction feature articles can use this same technique to establish a rhythm pattern. The process is simple: write the feature in an interesting way, but insert key "pitch" lines along the way to make it seem as though the reader is part of what's happening.

In Jon Franklin's Pulitzer-Prize-winning article, "Mrs. Kelly's Monster," Franklin presented the story of Mrs. Kelly's operation to have a tumor removed from her brain. As Franklin wrote the feature—which was fascinating in and of itself—he occasionally inserted a line that imitated the heart monitor:

"Pop, pop, pop."

It added tension and drama to the story when the inserted line started to change:

"Pop, pop, pop . pop . . pop . . . pop . . . . pop."

By doing this, the reader instantly realizes that the surgeon has done something that has put the patient's life in danger. The heart is slowing down. Mrs. Kelly is on the verge of dying. Uh-oh, what will happen next?

Obviously, Franklin's pitch line creates a lot of anxiety in the reader, causing him or her to read on, eager to discover what would happen next. However, a pitch line does not always have to be hyper-dramatic. It can also be used to create a mood, establish a setting, or clarify an incident.

I once was assigned to do a feature story every day for a week on the Indiana State Fair. Well, the first few days were easy. I interviewed visiting entertainers and dignitaries, I wrote about the judgings of everything from peach preserves to cattle, and I even did an article on quilting. By day seven, however, I had run out of ideas. So, I decided to write about all of the different people who run the food concession stands.

The feature part of the article discussed how carnies traveled from town to town, what volumes of food and drink were consumed in a day and a week, and how the food was preserved, prepared, and marketed. Interspersed among the paragraphs, however, I inserted italicized lines listing the various foods available at a state-fair midway

*"Cotton candy...taffy bars...popcorn...candy apples...."*

Three paragraphs later, I inserted another line:

*"Hot coffee...lemonade...orange drink...cold apple cider...."*

And so it continued until the end of the feature. The pitch lines created a sensation of walking down a state-fair midway and visually spotting all the different consumables being sold. It put the reader in the scene. Naturally, this technique should not be used too often. The effect will become tedious if it is overdone. As a change of pace, however, it can serve to woo the reader into the feature and to keep him or her involved. So, *hurry, hurry, hurry,* and give it a try.

**Terrific Technique Tip 3
Sharpen Your Prose with
These Four Poet Tips**

**Most poets convey** more of a message in 250 words than most prose writers do in 1,250 words. That's because poets select words for their maximum impact.

Poets are concerned about how a word sounds, how it meets the eye when read or the ear when spoken aloud, how its rhythm assists the flow of the rest of the sentence, and what its connotative as well as denotative meanings are. If you want to make your prose more vibrant and less wooden, try adapting some poetic techniques to your writing. Here are some suggestions:

1. **Begin by using alliteration.** By repeating a specific consonant, you can create a "sound effect" to mimic the object or scene you are describing. Without alliteration, you might write, "A lot of water can hit the beach during autumn." Notice, however, that with the repetition of eight "s" sounds in one sentence, you can create the sound of the ocean by writing, "The salty seas washed waves of spray onto the shores." It's impossible to read that sentence without hearing the whoosh and hiss of ocean waves rolling in and receding. That sound helps to put the reader into the setting.

2. **Experiment with vivid word pictures.** When poet Percy Shelley wrote: "I fall on the thorns of life! I bleed!" he was using graphic images to put the reader's senses on edge. In chapter 10 of *The Red Badge of Courage*, novelist Stephen Crane achieved the same effect (with prose) when he wrote, "[H]e could not keep his crime concealed in his bosom. It was sure to be brought plain by one of those arrows which cloud the air and are constantly pricking, discovering, proclaiming those things which are willed to be forever hidden." The image of Crane's arrows is as stark as the image of Shelley's thorns.

3. **Try using homonyms in a series.** Homonyms are words that sound exactly alike when pronounced, even though they have different spellings and meanings (rein, reign, rain… so, sew, sow). You can have fun creating homonym-linked sentences. In one of my romance novels I once had a pirate say, "Aye, I eyed 'em on yonder dock." I received several letters from readers who caught that play on words and enjoyed it.

Attempt to create some words that can have two meanings in one sentence. In Shakespeare's *Twelfth Night*, one character says, "The clock hath tolled twelve." When you hear that spoken by an actor, it can have three different meanings: (1) the clock clanged (tolled) twelve times; or (2) the clock, by chiming, "told" you it was twelve o'clock; or (3) the clock counted out twelve chimes, like a bank teller counts or "tolls" money. This gives extra mileage to the meaning of a word.

4. **Make use of similes.** A simile relates one thing to something else and usually uses the word "like" or "as" to compare the two. In his novel *Sanctuary*, William Faulkner writes in chapter 8, "Temple's head began to move . . . like one of those papier-mâché Easter toys filled with candy." If you've ever seen a Mexican piñata suspended from a string, slowly turning in a dangling twist, you immediately understand the movement Faulkner is referring to. Sentences of descriptive words could never explain that precise movement, but one comparison to the piñata enables the reader to see it right away. The next time you are at a loss for words in trying to explain something, try using a simile to liken your object to something the reader is already familiar with. It works…like clockwork. (See?)

Many of the world's most popular prose writers—Edgar Allan Poe, Thomas Hardy, Robert Louis Stevenson, Stephen Crane, William Shakespeare, James Dickey—have also been talented poets. We can learn a lesson from them. If a prose writer can select words with the same accuracy as a poet and can make use of some of the literary devices used by the poet, prose can then be as three-dimensional and as vivid as poetry.

So, give that latest manuscript of yours a bit more revision. Add the "poet's touch."

**Although I've written** plays, novels, short stories, devotions, articles, and even textbooks, the greatest reader response I've received has always been from my first-person articles.

Fifteen years after I came home from the Vietnam War, I wrote a 2,000-word feature titled, "Why I Fought in Vietnam, and Why I'd Do It Again." That article has been published in *The Baptist Bulletin*, *War Cry*, *The Waynedale News*, *Military Life*, and ten other magazines and newspapers. It also has been translated into German, Portuguese, and Russian for publication in international periodicals. It first ran in 1984 and most recently in 2013. I have stacks of letters from veterans who wrote to say, "You explained how I felt, but I just didn't know how to put it in words. I've shared your article with all my relatives and friends."

On the other end of the spectrum, I wrote a 1,900-word feature titled, "Funeral Planning Fun? Dead Right!" It was a satirical report about the bizarre ordeal my wife and I went through in buying caskets, ordering a tombstone, and planning our funerals. It was published in nineteen newspapers in early 2013, and I received e-mails and letters from readers who said, "I laughed so hard, I fell out of my chair. Who would have thought that the subject of death could have been so hilarious!"

These two examples—one extremely serious, the other totally comedic—show how much readers appreciate and become impacted by I-was-right-there narratives. But writing first-person articles is tricky because the finished product shouldn't read as though it's something you've extracted from your diary or copied from your personal journal. Readers don't give a rip about your summer vacation or your difficulties using new computers or your embarrassment at being overweight at your class reunion *unless they can receive some insight and personal benefit by reading the piece.*

## Bring the Reader Along

Begin writing your first-person narrative with the goal of revealing something of importance to the reader. It can be presented in a tongue-in-cheek manner, but it still has to make the reader say when finishing the piece, "Aha, so that's what it's like."

In essence, you will be taking the reader along with you to hear what you hear, see what you see, and feel what you feel. The reader, however, will be at a safe distance and will be able to laugh at you, cry with you, or discover along with you without actually having to fight in Vietnam, plan a funeral, or engage in whatever other episode you may wish to write about.

A word of caution: first-person narratives are not letters to the editor or complaints to the chamber of commerce. If you have an ax to grind, you'll lose readers immediately. Readers want anecdotes and stories, dialogue and scenes, a grabber opening and a fulfilling conclusion. If you mount a soapbox, you'll be there alone.

It is vital to show, not merely tell. You have to get the reader directly involved in what is going on. In my Vietnam piece, I used dialogue and description to let the readers sit in with me during my military enlistment, when having conversations with my army buddies during deployment, and later when talking with family members after coming back to America.

Readers witnessed events firsthand. They weren't presented a list of statistics, facts, and data; they were given a saga with a strong narrative drive that dealt with genuine human emotions and serious moral issues. Like it or not, they found themselves wondering, "What would I have done in a situation like that?"

Beginning writers worry that using the word "I" so many times will alienate readers. There is some truth in that. After all, suicide notes are written in first person. But what I've discovered is that if I make myself the fall guy in the narrative—I'm naïve and learning as I go along—readers will start pulling for me. They'll empathize with me, identify with me, and hope that I will survive the ordeal ultimately and be the better man for it. That's because by then, they are seeing themselves in the same circumstances.

## Finding the Material

Ideas for first-person articles can come from any number of personal experiences (going camping, visiting a nursing home, witnessing a robbery). Make a list of events and adventures in your life this past year, then ask if any topic is something you would want to help the reader avoid, help the reader cope with, help the reader learn about, or help the reader experience with you.

As you work on your first draft, do not use the inverted pyramid journalistic approach. That technique presents all the key facts very early in the story and then just tapers off with ancillary information. Instead, incorporate fiction-writing techniques.

For example, make sure you have a gripping lead. The opening for my Vietnam story was, "I have only seen my father cry twice. Once was at his mother's funeral. The other was the day I left for Vietnam." This obviously sets the tone as being serious, and it immediately lets the reader know that I will be telling my personal story.

Remember this: What's special about the first-person narrative is that it cannot be assigned by an editor. Your real-life experiences are unique. Additionally, the narrative will be told in the distinct voice of the writer, not merely some standardized 5-Ws verbiage. You'll need to establish a flow to your narrative, create a chronology of events that will each engage the reader's imagination, and build toward a boffo ending.

Although the first-person article is, in effect, your proclamation of "been there, done that," it won't impress readers until you can add "and now you can come, too, and you'll be glad you did!"

❖

## Terrific Technique Tip 5
## Reviving the Lost Art of
## Headline Writing

**During a writers**-conference Q&A time, a participant asked me, "If magazine and newspaper editors have the right to change our story and article titles, why should we bother trying to come up with ingenious headlines?" That question contained more than a hint of bitterness.

Yes, it is true that editors can—and often do—change the titles writers put on their articles and stories. To them, the title may be too long or too short for the page design. It may not have enough zip and punch, or it may not be aimed at the best target readership, or it may sound too much like another title in that issue. Editors don't need to justify *why* they change headlines.

Very often editors honestly believe they are *better* at writing headlines than freelance writers are. I once wrote an article about my father and his career of making artificial eyes. I submitted the article with the title, "The Eyes Have It," which I thought was a very witty pun. However, when the article was published, the editor had changed the headline to a phrase from the Bible: "An Eye for an Eye." To me, both were clever, but the editor always has the final say.

Let me share with you the answers I provided the person at the writers conference regarding why it is still necessary for writers to create captivating headlines for their manuscripts:

1. **It keeps the article on target.** As the writer, you need a bull's-eye to aim at. By writing a succinct, narrow-focused headline, you avoid topic detours and superfluous journalistic add-ons. You stick to the subject at hand. Anything that does not relate to that title will be cut.

2. **It presells the piece to the reader.** By creating a title that offers a solution to a problem or promises a better way of life or poses a question that piques reader curiosity, you enhance your chances of wooing an audience. Editors love that.

3. **It lifts your work from the slush pile.** Even if an editor decides later to modify your title, your original cleverness may be the very reason the editor bothered to read *your* manuscript amidst the hundreds of others submitted that year. If you can write a zinger of a headline, the editor will assume there's reason to believe the rest of the manuscript may also have merit. It'll be worth a look.

4. **Editors now need multiple titles.** A new style of journalism has arisen due to online publishing. Print publications used to have standard pages of three columns of print with one bold headline and, perhaps, one sidebar of added facts. Now online periodicals use numerous subtitles, bullet points, hot boxes, and inserts. Readers want short paragraphs, white space, and eye-grabbing subheadings. Writers can help editors by coming up with suggestions about where to break an article, how to subtitle the breaks, and even how to format the article. (Please note it's no accident this article has short paragraphs and subhead listings.)

5. **It stimulates your personal creativity.** Some writers prepare an entire article before deciding what it should be titled. However, I'm convinced that forcing the brain to create

a socko title will stimulate creativity. For example, one of my favorite challenges is to come up with a title that juxtaposes two opposites. One of my books was titled *Positive Workaholism*. A couple of my articles were titled, "Improve Your Marriage by Taking Separate Vacations" and "Having Fun Planning Your Funeral." Whatever writing exercise you choose to engage in, the creative energy you stimulate will spill over into the assignment itself.

So, whereas it is true that editors are in control of what will be the title, ultimately, for a published article or story, it is also true that editors appreciate help in developing titles. Writing excellent headlines provides discipline and creativity for the writer while saving time for the editor. It's the only title bout where both contenders come out as champs.

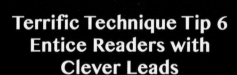

**Terrific Technique Tip 6
Entice Readers with
Clever Leads**

**A cartoon in** a national magazine showed a freelance writer on the phone with his editor. The writer, surrounded by crumpled papers, disheveled books, and a cup of spilled coffee is shouting into the mouthpiece, "But it really *was* a dark and stormy night."

And there you have it. You may be telling the truth, but if the lead to your article is bland, your editor will reject it—and probably the rest of the article with it.

In the late 1970s, when I was cutting my journalistic teeth as a young reporter for the *Muncie Star*, I was expected to investigate the news, get back to the office, and pound out the information on an electric typewriter in time for an early morning press run. That meant an article's lead didn't have to be flowery, just accurate and succinct. My editor expected the *who, what, when,* and *where* information, but he cared very little about the *why* or *how.*

Today, with online reporting, news-streaming, and media convergence, readers still want to be drawn immediately into a work of nonfiction, but they also expect more regarding the relational aspects of news. How will what is being reported impact their lives? Could such events or situations transpire in their sphere of day-to-day activities? What seems to be the national mood regarding this occurrence? Thus, today's lead must also set the tone for the story and establish the voice in which it will be shared. Tone and voice are especially true for people who read blogs, where elements of personal opinion or individual perspectives are frequently injected as part of the reporting or analyzing of events. Unlike previous generations, today's readers are curious about why the reporter decided to cover such an event and what his or her "take" on it is.

## In the Beginning

One of my early mentors used to say, "The trick to writing great articles is to focus on an interesting story that fascinates readers while also teaching them something they didn't know." With that in mind, I've always tried to locate the most captivating or inspirational or unique aspect of the material I've gathered about a topic and to use that key fact as my lead, presenting it in such a way that makes readers desire to absorb more about the subject. If, in drawing in the readers with my lead, I also can tickle, amaze, or surprise them, then all the better.

But it all begins with that initial enticement. A good lead works like lifting the top of a treasure chest and allowing readers to peek inside. If there is a promise of gold, the reader will plunge forth. It is then, matey, that the story must deliver the goods—an article that is properly researched, well organized, and informative. A clever lead will only anger readers if it is followed by a lame article.

I use certain leads frequently because they are reliable. Here are three of my favorites:

1. **Perplexing circumstances.** This lead introduces a nonthreatening character whom readers can identify with, but who has been confronted with an unexpected, potentially tragic situation. Her classic home is threatened with destruction to make room for a new expressway. His small herd of livestock will be put down unless a cure for the animals' disease can be found. Their fundraiser will be canceled unless they can convince the mayor to grant a parade license. The article must reveal how the persons being written about met the challenges and solved the problems. This serves as takeaway value for readers, who learn lessons vicariously.

2. **Juxtaposition of norms.** This lead requires you to show the main person of your article behaving in a radically abnormal manner for his or her position in life, and then explaining why and how this came about. I opened a story showing a school principal being spanked in his office by students. Turns out, it was for a promotional video about violence in schools. I opened another article by telling of a woman, who was terrified of heights, leaping off a bridge for a bungee jump. It turned out the bridge was only a projection on a screen, and the woman was only simulating the jump as a way of helping her confront her fear of heights while being in no actual danger.

3. **Comparison.** Most folks don't like to be confronted by a lot of math or statistics, but for some reason, they are fascinated by comparisons. I wrote an article once about a new Disney cruise ship, and the lead noted, "Being three times larger than the infamous *Titanic*, this cruise ship is not only a floating hotel but also the city that surrounds it."

In striving to create a good lead, look over your notes. Underline the best quotations, the most fascinating statistics, the oddest or most surprising facts about the matter, or any perplexing new viewpoint being offered. Then step back and examine what you've brought to your attention. Odds are, the lead will be in there somewhere. Snag it!

## Terrific Technique Tip 7
## All's Well That Ends Well

**Have you ever** spent three days reading a novel, and then the ending fell flat? Drives you nuts, doesn't it? Same thing with a movie or short story or even an article that proves to be a big disappointment.

When people talk about their favorite short stories or novels, they seldom choose works that are set apart by their leads. Most often, people love stories for the amazing way they end.

O. Henry's "The Gift of the Magi" and "The Ransom of Red Chief"; Jack London's "To Build a Fire"; Arthur Conan Doyle's "A Study in Scarlet"; and Agatha Christie's *The Mousetrap* all have surprising, yet logical endings that have caused people to talk about them for decades.

That didn't happen by accident. Hemingway told interviewer George Plimpton he rewrote the ending of *A Farewell to Arms* thirty-nine times before he felt he finally got it right.

During the past several decades, having written more than 160 published short stories and ten novels, I've discovered that a well-structured story usually leads to a satisfying ending. At times, I have been so concerned about the effectiveness of a story's conclusion, I have written the ending and then gone back and created the story that leads up to it. This helps because it is vital to foreshadow the story's outcome by giving inferences, clues, and subtle references throughout the tale. It's desirable to surprise the reader without using deceit or trickery. In many ways, a satisfying ending is a reflection of a story's beginning.

In teaching fiction to my university writing students, I assign them to come up with four different endings for the first short story they submit in my class. (Yes, I'll admit, I stole this idea from the movie version of the board game *Clue*, but, hey, it works.) I've discovered that each of the four endings gets more and more concise. That pleases me because I've never been a fan of cozy mysteries that end by having the detective assemble ten people in a room and then drone on for fifteen pages as to who could *not* have committed the murder before finally announcing who *did* commit the murder. Pul-ease! The days of melodrama are over, friends!

## The Focus of a Good Story

All stories need rhythm. Stories also need a compelling lead, some aspects of backstory, definite elements of character development, a compelling climax, and then a satisfying conclusion. Although the climax is usually the high point of the story, the denouement or resolution must leave the reader with a sense of fulfillment.

That's why I stress to my students that they remember a story is not a moment-by-moment chronology of a person's life (or joined persons' lives). It is a focus on a specific challenge or event or episode within that greater sphere. True, it may contain a panorama of circumstances that span several years and may even result in the death of the main character, but it is still a limited analysis of one primary episode within the grander scheme of all existence. We don't *have* to know all of the events in a character's life that led to this event (we have no idea what happened to Dorothy's parents in *The Wizard of Oz*), nor do we have to know all of the subsequent events that happen in a character's life *after* our story concludes (although we may be pretty convinced that Scarlett is going to hang on to Tara or that Huck is going to avoid getting adopted and socialized by the city folk).

## Some Cardinal Rules

Certain rules govern successful endings. The central character must make a right decision in the end, even if he or she has bungled most of the other decisions up to this point. The main character must grow in some aspect by having learned a lesson, gained a new perspective, or suffered in significant ways. The main character must have come off a climactic confrontation with a stunning adversary, endured a final battle of cataclysmic proportions, and arrived at a point at which an internal learning curve related to the essence of the story's main events has changed the central character in significant and obvious ways.

To achieve all of this, I jot down notes, scene ideas, and plot points (even for a short story) prior to commencing the writing. My thinking is, the buildup scenes should be like the softening-up blows in a boxing match, the climax should be the KO punch, and the conclusion should be the referee's ten-count pronouncement that "you're out."

I want to make sure my ending doesn't depend on a coincidence (although that is permissible for leads), that it doesn't present an unrealistic "happily ever after" scenario, and that it is not illogical or unrelated to the plot at hand. I also want to tie up all loose ends. Even books in a series (think *Harry Potter* and *Hunger Games* and *Anne of Green Gables*) have to have a sense of closure for each book's unit of tension and challenge in the overarching central plot that carries from one book to the next.

## Selling Your Next Book

Mickey Spillane once gave me this advice when I interviewed him: "The first chapter sells the book, and the last chapter sells the next book." Knowing this, make the last chapter something superb.

Endings in articles, features, and nonfiction books can also fail for a variety of reasons. Knowing how to recognize these problems will help you avoid them.

1. **Don't be redundant.** Reading a huge summary paragraph is tedious. If the reader has forgotten your key points, she can go back and read the article again. Thus, never write, "In

summary...." That may work well in some speeches, but it doesn't succeed in writing.

2. **Don't be elusive.** Write a definite ending that answers all questions, summarizes all matters, and leaves nothing to doubt. Nail it. Reread your manuscript, looking for holes, assumptions, speculations, or ambiguities. Either delete them or explain them, and then resolve each by the end of the manuscript.

3. **Don't be listless.** Don't just slow down, hit your required word count, and then stop. Drive to a designated ending, have a snappy closing paragraph and final line, and cause the reader to feel satisfied. Writing that great ending is why it is good to finish a manuscript several days before a deadline. Doing so allows you to mull for a day or two on how to create a gripping opening line and an equally socko ending. Never leave the readers bored or unfulfilled.

4. **Don't divert from your topic.** Don't start your article focused on one topic and then find yourself sliding into a related but non-pertinent aspect of that topic and then ending the article after talking about the secondary topic. Stay fixated on the primary topic all the way to the end.

For example, a student at a writers conference showed me her manuscript about powerboat racing through the Everglades. It started well by describing the difficult course, the design of the racing crafts, and the men doing the racing. However, somewhere in the middle of the article it drifted into a discussion of the protected wildlife of the Everglades (everything from crocodiles to flamingos to rare orchids), and the article concluded with a call for environmental protection. It never gave the details of the race or even mentioned who won it. Obviously, this was an article that was covering two totally different topics, despite the fact they both had a tie-in to the Everglades. Always stick to the topic at hand.

5. **Don't tell the reader how to think.** If the facts of your piece don't make a strong-enough case to validate your stance, it won't help to admonish your reader to vote Republican or join the union or attend the Baptist church or enlist in the Navy. When readers detect that you have become so prejudiced toward one side of your topic that you cannot write with an unbiased mind, they will lose confidence in your ability to discern truth, and they'll stop reading.

6. **Don't exaggerate or lie.** If you are writing nonfiction, and the ending of your article or interview or feature is sad, disappointing, or aggravating, don't modify the truth to have it fit the happily-ever-after conclusion you would prefer. Don't sacrifice your journalistic integrity just so you can draw a happy face after your final sentence. Life is what it is.

Shakespeare was correct when he titled a play *All's Well That Ends Well*. Work diligently on getting the ending of your story as nearly perfect as possible. When you do that, editors—and readers—will want to read your next one.

# Chapter 3
# Getting Unstuck

> **Getting Unstuck Tip 1**
> **Been Rejected?**
> **Join the Club**

**Even though I** had a successful writing career of four decades, one of my books got rejected by nine publishers before my agent placed it with a well-respected house. Coping with rejection is an unfortunate part of the business of professional writing. Here are five ways to make it less painful:

1. **Understand What Rejection Is.** Rejection is one editor rejecting one manuscript on one day. It is not a ruling that you have no talent. Maybe the editor was wrong and didn't realize how good your manuscript was. Maybe she had a fight with her spouse that morning and was in such a foul mood she rejected everything. Maybe something in your manuscript was potentially offensive to one of the publication's advertisers, or the publication put a freeze on new purchases because of cash-flow problems, or the editor recently received a story or article covering your topic.

Keep in mind that although writing involves an extension of the self, *you* were not rejected. Your manuscript was, and it's not always about a lack of talent.

2. **Keep Producing New Work.** Getting published is an odds game, so keep producing new work and get as much in the mail as possible. Nothing ever sold by being left on a computer, never having been submitted. If something is rejected, odds are that one of your other fifteen pieces will get accepted. If something is accepted, you won't get a big head because odds are one of your other fifteen pieces will get rejected.

   But don't dwell on rejection. Go back to your writing. Revise and resubmit. Try a different market. Be persistent. Be glad sometimes that material does get rejected if it turns out you were in too much of a hurry to have done a quality job.

3. **Fix the Problems.** Since editors want to accept manuscripts—because that's what keeps them in business—it imperative that you find out why they aren't accepting *your* manuscripts so you can fix the problem.

   If four editors say your work is too wordy or too shallow in research or too narrow in market appeal, heed that collective advice and revise accordingly. If you are told that you lack depth in understanding the genre in which you desire to write, take time to read works in that genre, discuss them with other writers, and attend sessions at a writers conference about writing for that genre (or age group or target market).

   If the mechanics of your writing are weak, hire a book doctor or copyeditor who not only will proofread and edit your pages but also will explain to you what a split infinitive is, how the ellipsis should be typed, and when to use dashes instead of commas.

4. **Don't Sabotage Your Own Efforts.** Some writers invite rejection through negative behavior. For example, if you get a rejection letter but the editor says "try us again" or "send more,"

you would be a fool not to jump on that opportunity. Also, if your method of marketing has been a shotgun approach—you simply send out manuscripts at random—start analyzing markets more carefully and targeting publications that truly need what you are writing about.

If you've been going solo and getting rejections, join a writers group and seek feedback and comments. If there is something truly wrong with your writing and you cannot fix it, then seek someone who can. Learn to accept criticism.

Consider editorial requirements, too. You absolutely must read a publication's writers guidelines and adhere to them. You must send a dazzling query letter since that's the gateway for the presentation of your actual manuscript. And you must have a powerful style of presenting your message. I've known writers who can write flawless pages, never making errors in grammar, syntax, spelling, format, or punctuation. The problem is, they either say nothing of significance, or what they say is dull, slow, boring, or tedious.

5. **Realize You're Not Alone.** Every writer knows the bitter taste of rejection. It's part of the process of getting better at the craft. For instance, Davis Bunn is a best-selling novelist, but he admits that the first six novels he wrote were never published. He stayed at it because he considered himself a novice, not a failure.

Holly G. Miller, formerly an editor at *The Saturday Evening Post*, sold one article early her career and then had more than a dozen rejections before making a second sale. She discovered that "fool luck" needed to be replaced by serious study of how to write and market manuscripts.

So, if you are getting rejection slips, you're not alone. However, there are steps to take to reduce the number of rejections you receive. Instead of allowing rejection letters to defeat you, use them as prods to get better. In time, you'll be able to reject the rejections by getting published.

---

## Getting Unstuck Tip 2
## Benefit from Bromides

---

**Probably the first** rule writing instructors drilled into us was to avoid clichés, those overused, worn-out, tired expressions heard so frequently in daily conversations. However, the only way an expression can become overused is if it contains enough truth to warrant being repeated.

Knowing this, let's reexamine some of the tried and true clichés that relate to overcoming procrastination and managing time in order to find out how they might jumpstart our writing.

1. **Time and tide wait for no man.** Magazines have ironclad lead times for their issues. If a publication's guidelines say that all Christmas articles must be submitted no later than August 15, you'll have to hit that deadline or you'll lose that publication opportunity for another full year. Editors and deadlines wait for no one.

   Similarly, book publishers work on catalog seasons. If you plan to have your novel among a company's summer releases, you'll have to have everything done six months earlier (including the proofreading and correcting of galleys). Bookstore owners and readers wait for no idlers. So hit your deadlines in all matters.

53

2. **Inch by inch, anything's a cinch.** Often we hesitate to start working on large projects because they seem overwhelming. But if we break a big job into smaller components, it will become more manageable.

   When it came time for me to research and write my 325-page doctoral dissertation, I panicked. However, when the chairman of my committee told me to break it into twelve chapters and then divide each chapter into four feature-length subdivisions, I could see it would be no different from writing one magazine article per week. I could—and did—handle that. You can too. So break your big project into smaller units.

3. **The longest journey begins with a single step.** In my last year of high school, I determined that I wanted to make writing my career. In fact, I fantasized about cracking the *New York Times* best-seller list, writing Hollywood scripts, and hobnobbing with members of the literati. In time (read that *decades*), all that came to pass. What I discovered along the way, however, was that there were no quantum career leaps. Everything came one step at a time: college student, newspaper reporter, short-story writer, soldier, graduate student, columnist, novelist, editor, screenwriter, college professor. The same is true of your career. So step out. Today!

4. **He who hesitates is lost.** Either by direct effort or mere luck, some plum writing assignments will fall into your lap from time to time. If you waste time worrying about whether or not you are ready to handle such assignments—enough education? enough experience? enough time? enough publishing savvy?—you'll talk yourself out of taking what might well be your breakthrough gigs. Always say yes. To quote Woody Allen, "Eighty percent of success is showing up." Trust in your ability to learn as you earn. Go for it!

5. **Well begun is half done.** Physicists talk about the power of inertia. A body in motion tends to remain in motion. Well, apply that fact to getting started on your writing project. Initiate momentum by assembling all of your tools—notes, pens,

cup of java, file folders, recorded interviews. Clear away any distractions, e.g., magazines, books, unrelated research. Divide the work project into a series of stages. Go to the computer, and power it up. You're halfway home already.

6. **The race does not always go to the swift.** If you balk at starting a writing project because you know you are a plodder rather than a sprinter, take heart. Often the writer who dashes off a first draft and then rushes it to an editor winds up receiving it back with a rejection slip or request for additional research, better fact-checking, and improved writing. You, however, may take a bit longer to prepare your manuscript, but the high-quality end product will save you time overall. So get started, work at your own pace, and take home the blue ribbon when you cross the finish line.

Consider this parting thought: Solomon, the wisest man who ever lived, spent a lifetime assembling the book of Proverbs. Ben Franklin collected all the known one-liners and clichés of his era when he wrote *Poor Richard's Almanac*. Let a word to the wise be sufficient.

## Getting Unstuck Tip 3
## Beat the Self-Inflicted
## Isolation Blues

**Riding the success** of two best-selling books, I quit my nine-to-five job and stepped into life as a full-time freelance writer.

I set up a nice office at home. I slept late, worked in my pajamas if I wanted, drank a lot of coffee, and enjoyed living at the keyboard. Sometimes I'd get rolling and write all afternoon and night. I was my own boss. This was freedom. I was a lone wolf. I loved it…for about two months.

Then I got lonely. My wife and two children were the only people I saw daily, and they were usually gone. There were no chats at the water cooler, no gossip exchanges in the mailroom…not even kibitzing with an administrative assistant. This was decades ago, before the Internet and e-mail. I had cut myself off from society!

My writing suffered. I wasn't getting news of what people were interested in. I had no one to bounce my ideas off of, and no one was available for brainstorming. I hadn't heard a new joke in eight weeks. I needed to get out, but I didn't dare jeopardize my pattern of producing a set number of words each day.

By experiment and adaptation, I discovered several ways to maintain out-of-office contact without disrupting my writing schedule.

1. **Teaching Courses** – I discovered that the YMCA, the local library, and several area colleges were interested in weekly writing classes I could conduct. This got me out of the house every Thursday night for three hours and put some pay in my pocket. More importantly, it gave me a chance to sharpen my editing skills by critiquing the work of novices. And I benefited from their feedback on my projects (which I frequently read to the class).

2. **Coauthorship** – I approached Holly G. Miller, another full-time writer, with the idea of collaborating. Though we lived one-hundred miles apart, we talked to each other by sending cassette tapes when we exchanged manuscript pages. We co-authored four novels and three nonfiction books. We met face-to-face only a couple of times each year and talked by phone about every three months. Still, that outside contact supported my writing career. Today, e-mail, instant messaging, and Skype

make it even easier—if you can discipline yourself so they don't cut into your writing time.

3. **Working Out**—My wife convinced me that joining a health club would benefit me physically and socially. I made it a habit to drive to a health club for exercise, mild weightlifting, and then a refreshing shower. I'd usually do this mid-afternoon to break up the monotony of a full day of writing. Sometimes on a treadmill I'd talk to the people next to me. Other times I'd get on a stair-stepper and listen to an audio book.

4. **Library Visits** – I limited myself to two library visits each week—each time for research only. But I'd also ask the librarians what topics were hot that week. Sometimes I'd wander into the children's department and chat with students and teachers. I'd go to the video section and ask people what good or bad movies they'd seen and what they'd recommend and why. Not only were these talks fun, but they also gave me insight into what people were interested in. As a writer, I needed that.

5. **Writers Groups** – I joined two professional associations that held annual conventions where I could network with editors, agents, publishers, journalists, screenwriters, and novelists. I also joined a local writers club. It met only once a month, but the focus was usually interesting: a lawyer discussing copyright-law changes, a newspaper reporter explaining how syndication works, or a librarian suggesting shortcuts to historical research.

Although writing is best accomplished in solitude, writers are often social. If we weren't curious about people and events, we'd never have become writers. The trick is to strike a balance between socializing and work.

With today's technological opportunities, you may feel less isolated. Still, nothing beats face-to-face meetings. A handshake, a smile, a look of surprise, an impromptu question…some things can be experienced only in person.

As a writer who's discovered the value of coming out of hiding, I hope that never changes.

---

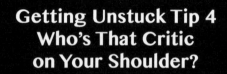

**Getting Unstuck Tip 4
Who's That Critic
on Your Shoulder?**

**The television crime** drama series *Perception* focused on a university professor who had done so much research on brain functioning, he actually could no longer trust his own brain. He self-analyzed every situation, even to the point of talking to imaginary people who seemed real to him. It made him come off both as a brilliant lecturer and as a delusional wacko.

I think most of us in the writing field have lives very much like this, although we would never admit it out loud. As we write our articles and novels, we hear "voices." Sometimes it's our ninth-grade English teacher telling us, "Not another comma splice! You know better!" Or it can be our mom saying, "Do you really have to write about *that* topic? Why not choose something less revealing, less private." Or it can be from someone in our critique group opining, "You're churning out another romance? I thought this was your year to flex your writing talent and go mainstream." Or it could be—and this is the one that always surprises me—a character in a story saying boldly, "Are you kidding? Why in the world would I say *that* and behave like *that*?"

Right now you probably are feeling less neurotic, just knowing that Doc Hensley also hears "voices." Of course I do. We all do. No writer creates out of a void or vacuum. But knowing which voices to listen to and which to ignore is where the professionalism—and sanity—takes over.

## Now Hear This...or Not

I honestly believe that wordsmiths can suffer from writer's block if they fail to have enough voices talking to them. If you, for example, are not getting feedback from a writers critique group or from folks at a writers conference, you're not getting new perspectives and fresh ideas for your books and articles. You need a second (or fifth) set of eyes on your manuscript to continue stimulating your creative process and to protect you from making errors where you are weak.

It isn't crazy to sort out who the valid and invalid voices are that you currently hear as you work. Take action to delete the negative voices. If, for instance, the high-school English teacher's voice keeps coming in, then you probably know subconsciously that you're having serious problems with the mechanics of writing. Okay, solve that problem. Once you're finished with your first draft, hire a private proofreader/copyeditor. He or she can clean up your mechanical problems, as well as teach you how to avoid them in the future. Good! That's one negative voice gone!

Similarly, if the voice of your mother is your conscience testing you as to whether you might do harm to others by revealing a tragic incident from your past, confront that problem as well. Call your mom and say what you intend to do and how you feel it will be beneficial to others to learn how you coped with that tragedy. Get her to release you from guilt. If she says she feels it's too personal, write the story anyway, but change the locales, people's names, and the dates. The incident will still be pertinent and helpful. Okay, good, a second negative voice is now gone!

Continue to check off the voices that are stalling your creative momentum. Deal with the issues that cause these voices to pervade your writing time. Get rid of them. Afterward, go back to your list and start to draw positive encouragement from the voices that may be helping you.

Personally, I *like* to talk to people in my books. If one asks, "Doesn't this go against how I usually react to situations like this?" I will be forced to say, "Yes, you're right. But I need some new energy from you so readers won't predict ahead of time what you're going to do and say."

Sometimes I turn the tables and ask the character, "How can we plant an event in your childhood that will justify some suddenly surprising behavior by you as an adult?" This forces me to review what we've already established as the backstory for this character and to see where some additional experiences can be inserted. Since no one knows your fictional characters better than you do, who's the best-qualified person to speak on their behalf?

I have co-authored books with several other writers. So, sometimes I like to infuse their voices into the project I'm currently working on. When Stanley Field and I coauthored *The Freelancer* (Poetica Press), he would always ask, "Can we trim this? Can we tighten it? Can we focus it better?" So, I let Stan speak to me when I am proofreading my chapters.

When Holly G. Miller and I co-authored our novel *The Gift* (Harvest House), she would continually say, "But are you showing it from both a male and female perspective?" Women generally like details, emotional reactions, and relational moments, whereas men prefer bottom-line solutions, fast pacing, and solid logic. I try to maintain that balance when I hear Holly's voice.

Pamela Rice Hahn and I co-authored *Teach Yourself Grammar and Style in 24 Hours* (Macmillan). Pam was forever saying, "But have you verified those facts? Do you have collaborating sources? Is the research solid?" So, even when writing fiction, I hear her voice, and I make sure my locales are described correctly, and my dates are accurate.

## The Voice of Reason

As a writer, you'll discover that myriad people will try to invade your mind. Some will be supportive helpers, and others will be noisome detractors. It's your responsibility to be proactive in casting out the demon voices and welcoming the angelic ones.

And, if you ever have your doubts about being able to do it, just remember the voice of Doc Hensley who said, "I have faith in you."

---

## Getting Unstuck Tip 5
## Rev Up Your Brain to
## Conquer the Blank Page

**Forget all of** those stupid scenes in old-time movies wherein the tortured novelist is seated in front of his manual typewriter staring at a blank piece of paper. He takes a swallow of booze, pulls a long drag on his cigarette, runs a hand over his three-day-old growth of beard, and then furiously begins to pound the keys.

Likewise, forget all those stupid scenes in modern movies, such as *Limitless*, in which the tortured novelist sits in front of his computer, swallows a magic pill, runs a hand over his three-day-old growth of beard, and then furiously begins to pound the keys.

No elixirs or stimulants can be swallowed as a way of writing a best-seller. That's fiction, folks, and bad fiction at that. (Although I confess I keep a can of Diet Coke close at hand whenever I'm writing.)

So, what does work? I mean, let's be honest. We don't always arrive at the keyboard with smiles on our faces, bursting with brilliant concepts and ideas waiting to be birthed. More often than not, we wonder why we didn't take up a safe profession, such as alligator wrestling or being shot out of a cannon. We need ways to force our brilliance to come forth.

So, let's look at some methods worth your experimentation to rev up your brain.

1. **Do a timed writing session.** Set a timer for ten minutes. Attack your writing with a vengeance. Type out whatever comes to mind, whether dialogue or setting or backstory. Don't be concerned with writing mechanics. Just churn out as many words as possible before that timer sounds. Once the dinger goes off, relax, take a deep breath, and refill your coffee cup.

   Now that the right side of your brain has had a chance to vent, take time to allow the left side to check for grammar, spelling, syntax, and punctuation errors. Let it insert smoother transitions, better choices of vocabulary, and more natural conversations. This method works because you are using both sides of the brain as each was created to function.

2. **Consider the audience first.** Pick up a notepad and jot down responses to such key questions as, "Who, specifically, is my reader? Which periodicals or publishers are most likely to want this kind of manuscript? What sort of takeaway value will they expect from my material? How can I best meet those expectations?" Once you are clear on whom you are writing for and what you want to say and how you want to say it, the words will come more naturally.

3. **Prepare an outline.** If your notes and research materials are scattered around you, impose some discipline on that chaos. Make an outline of what you want to present. What needs to go into the lead to make it grab the reader? Which statistics or quotations or breakthrough announcements need to be presented early to hold the reader's interest? What factors

could be pulled together to make a satisfying and compelling close to the piece? Assemble these sections of your research and add this meat to the skeleton you've formulated.

4. **Brainstorm format options.** Consider three to five different ways you could write your article or story. Would a Q&A format be functional? Would a series of anecdotes strung together engage the reader? Would quotations from a variety of interviews provide insights and surprises? Would bullet points be eye-appealing? Should some of the material be segregated into a sidebar or hot box or banner? Could you devise a reading list or some quizzes or a compilation of supportive Scripture verses? By allowing yourself the freedom to visualize the manuscript in an array of presentations, you open possibilities for how to begin, continue, and conclude your piece.

5. **Write out of sequence.** Don't feel locked into a linear pattern of writing. When composing novels, I very often will write the opening chapter, and then I'll write the closing chapter. In this way, I know for sure what the problem is that will drive the plot, and I also know I can successfully bring it to a satisfying conclusion. The rest of the book is a series of action scenes, blind alleys, red herrings, comic relief, and dramatic exchanges of dialogue. Those scenes I write as I think of them, whether they are in chapter 2 or chapter 9.

6. **Put your brain in overdrive.** Lie on the couch, lean your head back toward the floor, and let oxygen-filled blood flow into your brain for a few minutes. Take ten minutes to work a crossword puzzle, decipher an anagram, or solve a section of Sudoku. Get on your knees and pray.

7. **Create a regimen.** Try to report to the same place at the same time each day for your writing. If you create a pattern, it will become a stimulus-and-response procedure. Just as your saliva and stomach acids increase when you sit for dinner, so also your memory and instinct and imagination will kick in when you sit to do your writing.

8. **Enlist a cohort.** If you have a writing partner or buddy, give him or her a call and say, "Let me read you something, and you tell me how this can be improved." Similarly, you might want to e-mail one or two pages of a work in progress and ask your writing friend to offer some feedback via Track Changes. Sometimes a different perspective can provide fresh ideas to what is becoming drudgery to you.

Staring at a flashing cursor is not productive. Yes, you must report to your writing desk. However, if nothing is coming naturally, then use the above techniques to kick your brain into gear. Nobody calls you creative until you've created something.

<hr/>

## Getting Unstuck Tip 6
## Trick Yourself into
## Working Faster

**When I was** in undergraduate school, I worked a couple of years for the college newspaper. Another guy my age who also worked for the paper wrote some fantastic features. His writing had wit, grace, organization, narrative flow, and a masterful use of vocabulary. The problem was, the guy was such a perfectionist, he could never meet a deadline. As a result, he was first taken off the news beat and restricted to features. Later, he was dropped from the staff entirely, being deemed a better fit for the *annual* literary magazine. Perfectionists don't fit well into the world of journalism.

My buddy Jerry B. Jenkins, author of more than 180 books, frequently tells a story about when he was the junior editor of a Sunday school take-home paper published by Scripture Press. It was Jerry's desire—his personal goal—to turn in a manuscript to senior editor Stan Baldwin that was so flawless, Stan could make no editorial changes or improvements to it. In four years at that job, Jerry never accomplished his mission. Stan always found sentences he could delete or a better word choice or a snappier lead. Said Jerry, "My goal was perfectionism, which proved to be impossible. However, I kept churning out material at a steady pace, knowing that the work had to continue."

That, friends, is the secret of success for writers. Yes, we should always strive to write the finest manuscripts possible, but we cannot spend days and weeks agonizing over every word and sentence, wondering if we have achieved a level of nirvana. The work has to go forth.

## Understanding Perfectionism

Unlike sculpturing, brain surgery, and high diving, writing isn't something that has to be done perfectly the first time out. In fact, a second draft of a manuscript usually adds the polish needed to make an ordinary piece of writing become something dynamic (read that as *publishable*). So, get it down, and *then* get it right.

Perfectionists worry too much about exhaustive research. At some point, you have to declare that the digging and probing and interviewing and note-taking are done, and it's time to do the writing.

I, myself, once had this problem. I spent four years researching the life and work of author Jack London in preparation for writing my doctoral dissertation. Each time I would think my dissertation was complete, some new book or article would come out about Jack London, and I would feel obligated to read it and make reference to it in my dissertation. Finally, my committee chairman said, "You're *done*, Hensley. I'm tired of meeting with you. Write the words 'the end,' and prepare to defend your dissertation." He was right. I could have dabbled with that research endlessly. Instead, I defended *my* research and received my doctorate. Enough, already!

Perfectionists cannot please themselves, because they often lack a clear focus. Even when a sentence or paragraph is a marvelous piece of creativity and logic, if the writer has no clue where it fits into the greater scheme of things, writing it has been a waste of effort. It is better to take some time to jot notes about the beginning, middle, and end of an article or story. What is the objective of the piece: To inform? To entertain? To analyze? To report? To critique? How will the material be presented: By statistics? By anecdotes? By interview quotations? Who will be the target audience: Teens? Senior citizens? Professionals? Laypeople? Some preplanning helps assure that the manuscript will stay on track, meet its objectives, and be properly organized.

Perfectionists get bogged down because they listen to the infernal internal editor. Perhaps line-by-line scrutiny is vital in the creation of a poem, but for prose writing, it's necessary to keep the fingers moving across the keyboard, drawing upon all the great material stored in the mind. As I tell my college students, "You can't edit a blank screen." Don't worry about flawless syntax and smooth transitions and whether to use a semicolon or a dash. Just get the first draft pounded out. Then let it sit a while, and later go back with fresh eyes and polish it.

Remember: *churn, spurn, burn, and earn.* Churn out ideas, spurn the internal editor, burn up pages with finished material, and earn bylines and bucks.

## Confronting Perfectionism

If you are a card-carrying perfectionist, you can trick yourself into working faster. One idea is to write your lead and your closing first. If you discover a great way to start, that'll create momentum. If you are confident you can conclude the piece well, you won't be in a panic about where the manuscript is going and when and how it should end.

Another trick is to speak the piece into an audio recorder. Just share the information in a logical, natural way. You then can transcribe your recording as a first draft. After that, you can revise and polish the material so that it is as effective when seen by the eye as it was when heard by the ear.

You can experiment with many other tricks. For example, set a clock for ten minutes and write like a maniac until the alarm goes off. You won't have time to be a perfectionist. Or, you can create an outline and then build your article or story step by step, allowing each segment to pass your perfectionist's inspection while you maintain steady momentum. Or, as with the Jenkins-Baldwin example, you can write the best manuscript possible but run it by someone else just to make sure it is perfect.

The lesson here is that striving for perfection is not wrong. However, being stymied by a compulsion to produce perfection is counterproductive. Keep in mind, when the readers see our published material, they won't know if it's a first draft or a fifth draft. And we aren't telling!

---

### Getting Unstuck Tip 7
### Making Work Less Tedious
### When It's Time to Churn Words

**I have a muse.** It's called terror. It was especially motivating when I was a full-time freelancer for fifteen years with a family to support. I'd get up on Monday and say, "The mortgage is due Friday. Churn words." I'd get up on Tuesday and say, "The kids need new shoes for Easter. Churn words." I'd get up on Wednesday and say, "We need groceries. Churn words." I'd get up on Thursday and say, "The heck with this. I'm tired of churning words," and my wife would say, "Quit clowning around. Go churn words." So, I would.

But, just how does one go about churning words? For me, it began with prep work. Long before Dr. Atul Gawande wrote his best-seller *The Checklist Manifesto* (Henry Holt, 2009), I had a checklist system that was every bit as rigorous as an airline captain's. I would go to my office and make sure that I was prepared to work that day: phone answering machine turned on for no disturbances, computer on standby, adequate paper in printer, wastebasket emptied, pencils sharpened, pads of paper on desk, drapes drawn to block out distractions, reference materials at ready reach, mug of coffee handy, and to-do list current and prioritized.

There was a psychological value in "going to work," even if it was a home office. After going through this checklist, I was ready for takeoff.

Next, I strove for closure on something small. I'd take the first hour to write two short devotions and send them to a publication, or I'd complete my Saturday column for the local newspaper, or I'd write a book review. I needed this, personally. These were small assignments, but they paid *something*, and starting my day by making money as a writer (any amount) gave my family cash flow and verified that I was a working professional. It also got my mind in gear, warming up for more taxing assignments.

After that, I'd take what I called a "working break." I'd get a second cup of coffee and spend an hour going through the mail. I'd take each new magazine and rip out the articles I felt would be useful and interesting, and I'd throw the rest away. I'd read a couple of articles, with a highlighter in hand to draw attention to key information, and then I'd either toss each article or file it in a cabinet for future reference. I'd then stack any incoming bills in one pile so my wife could pay them. Any payment checks that might have arrived that day would go with that pile for her to deposit into our bank account. I'd then review rejected manuscripts or accepted queries, assign each a project date and deadline, and place them atop a bookcase in order of pending priority work.

## Now the Big Stuff

Having earned some money and having attended to the day's correspondence, I would then focus on something monumental. I would stay focused on one writing project and move it as far forward as possible. If I was working on a short story, I'd stay at it for two hours. If it was a novel, I'd concentrate on a single chapter. If it was an interview assignment, I'd transcribe my tapes and start working on the first draft of the profile. To the best of my ability, I would not let anything interrupt me until time for lunch. I'd then be ready for a physical and mental break. Writing is draining, folks.

After a modest lunch, I'd stay away from the office for a couple of hours. I'd go to the basement and exercise on the treadmill or stationary bike and then shower and shave.

Perhaps I would do some pleasure reading. I might make phone calls, maybe watch a little bit of TV, or do yard work. Around 3:45 p.m. my two kids would come home, and I'd help them with homework, run them to the library or sports practices, and we'd all have dinner together.

Later in the evening, I would go back to my office for another three hours. Why, you may ask, did I break the day into two parts? Well, first, because I was brain-fried after four hours of office work. Second, I had to attend to other functions and responsibilities in life. And third, I needed distance from what I'd done that morning.

Once back in the office at night, I would start to edit the work I'd written that morning. I'd read it aloud. I'd copyedit it. I'd double-check facts and name spellings and statistics and quotations. If fiction, I'd act out scenes, checking the stage movements and listening to the dialogue. Sometimes my work was so brilliant, I'd produce seven pages of print-ready material. Other times it was so horrific, I'd scrap almost all of it. But even the pitched material got me closer to the end product. To sell words, you have to churn words. Continually.

## Dealing with Grunt Work

I constantly tell my college students that a bad day writing is better than a good day working at a fast-food restaurant. However, that does not mean I love every writing job I am offered. Sometimes we writers have to take whatever assignment comes along. Or perhaps we have a job in which we have to wear a lot of writer's hats. Such was the case when I was Public Information Officer at a small private college for four years. I was sports information coordinator, alumni magazine editor, student newspaper advisor, campus publicist, and senior public relations liaison.

I've learned a few tricks to make grunt work less tedious, and a big part of it begins with attitude. When I had to generate a feature article about the lacrosse team (a sport I hardly understood) or write a profile about a ninety-year-old alumnus who had died and left money to build a new library for our school (but was somebody I'd never even met), I'd tell myself, "Okay, this isn't as much fun as writing a novel, but it pays the bills and puts food on the table. Do your work, and be happy you have a job *as a writer*." I'd dig in and get the piece written.

## It Always Can Be Interesting

Another thing that made grunt writing more palatable was knowing the secret of why people bothered to read articles. They wanted to be entertained or taught something. In short, they desired takeaway value. They wanted to feel that the time they had spent reading an article had been worth it because it had amused them or had enlightened them in some way.

What this meant to me was, if I was assigned to write a profile, I couldn't prepare it like an obituary: birthday, education, marriage, military service, career, death. Ugh! No, instead, I had to discover, either by research or by interviewing, the insights this person could pass along to others. How did she get rich? How did he train for that Olympic medal? What was the trick for creating so many new patents? This became fun for me, too, because I had to probe, question, and dig. After discovering the gems, the writing part became easy.

Another challenge was to find ways to make any subject comprehensible to lay readers. Imagine, for example, that I had to prepare an article about a mathematics professor who had made a breakthrough in quantum physics or in wind power or in outer-space navigation. Mention math to most people, and they run for the hills.

So, rather than filling my article with a string of numbers towing lots of zeroes, I would dream up comparisons—just like I counseled the community college math professor to do, as I mentioned earlier. For instance, instead of saying that a new energy-efficient windmill was 3,627 inches tall, I would say, "After being pieced together and pulled erect, this behemoth was as high as a football field is long." You don't have to have a PhD in math in order to picture that dimension in your mind's eye.

Likewise, in describing new compression elements for an iPad or Nook, I wouldn't talk about 727 feet of shelf space in a library. I'd say, "A collection of hardbound books that could fill your two-car garage can now be contained within a digital reader that is the size and weight of *one* book." That hit home to most folks.

The very nature of a publication's theme or topic can immediately intimidate certain readers. If I picked up a sports magazine and didn't understand sports lingo, I'd be wary of my ability to find value in this publication's articles. Or, if I had never studied to be a pilot, an air-navigation magazine would seem daunting to understand. Such was my challenge in editing a college alumni magazine. Some readers instantly feared that it would contain a collection of mega-brainy articles written from a professorial perspective. In short, they assumed its material would be boring, incomprehensible, and narrow.

Knowing this, I avoided fifty-cent vocabulary and opted for common terms—not "sociological inter-connective cognitive inter-personalization" but "showing folks how to relate to others on equal terms." I'd paraphrase what the professors told me so as to reduce equations and theories and experiments down to amusing anecdotes or illustrative examples. I'd see if I could include drawings or simplified charts or photos that made abstract concepts seem more concrete, more visual, more apparent.

To be able to do this, I'd often have to spend many hours with the professors, making sure I truly understood what in the world they were talking about before I attempted to "translate" it into street talk. When I'd run my article by them a day or two later, many of them would say, "Hey, give me a copy of that. I have to deliver a paper on this next month, and that'll make it easier for me to explain things to my audience."

## Thinking First of the Readers

The reason grunt work often seems laborious is because it requires a precision that imaginative writing does not demand. It forces writers to get on the other side of the desk and become the readers. They must create clever, informative, exciting ways of explaining what seems to be either incomprehensible or inapplicable to the average person's life.

It's hard. It's challenging. But it's rewarding. One professor told me she used an article I had written about her research as part of an application for a grant. She laughed and said, "The governing board members said they couldn't make head or tail of what I'd written in my proposal, but after reading your article about what my research was accomplishing, they saw the value in funding it. I got the money."

So, keep in mind, it's only grunt work when you forget to instill the magic and wisdom. Using my system to churn words, I was happy overall. And some days, such as when I saw my photo on the back cover of a new book or one of my pieces was made the cover story of a national magazine or I received a fan letter from someone who "absolutely loved" something I'd written, then I was euphoric.

I don't think that's an emotion I would experience as a fast-food worker simply churning out burger orders.

# Chapter 4
# Being a *Creative* Writer

**I know two** things for sure about creativity. First, no one creates out of a vacuum. Until you put something in, you can't get something out. Second, you cannot edit a blank page. Creative or not, you still have to pound out a certain number of words each day, which means that creativity is useless without discipline.

Let me explain. Our brains are divided into two functional spheres. The right side is La-La Land, where we daydream, experiment with patterns, form bizarre images, create random color combinations, engage in humorous word play, and delve into the abstract and ambiguous. The left side is Boot Camp, where we are disciplined with numbers, sequential in organization, logical in analysis, and precise with vocabulary usage.

Unfortunately, these two spheres are often at odds with each other. The right side is like the joystick on an airplane, pulled all the way back, zooming us into sky-high realms of imagination and exploration.

The left side is like the autopilot switch that forces the ailerons into a downward dive while applying the air brakes. We need both creativity and critical thinking, but how do we get these divergent gifts to work in tandem?

## Coordinating Creativity's Four Phases

When facing a creative challenge as an author—outlining a novel, drafting a keynote address for a writers conference, crafting a short story—professionals engage in a four-stage development process.

1. They conduct research by gathering facts, quotes, data, references, and background on the topic they wish to write about.

2. They incubate this material by reading it, organizing it into sequential patterns, jotting down questions about unsolved areas, and mulling about problem points. Grandpa used to call this "sleeping on it."

3. As creative insights or bursts of inspiration arise, professional authors quickly jot them down without prejudging whether they are practical or not. These are the breakthrough moments that will provide unique, fascinating, unusual potential solutions to the challenges at hand.

4. At the proper time, these authors apply the discipline of analyzing how to formulate these "ah-ha" epiphanies into material that is coherent, captivating, and insightful.

## Turning Plots into Published Stories

My success as a short-story writer and novelist can be reduced to a three-step procedure: come up with a fascinating plot, bang out the first draft of the story as soon as possible, and spend serious time editing, proofreading, and revising that lame initial effort.

I learned a long time ago that most people are really very creative. If, like me, most folks watch TV, go to the movies, read books, listen to sermons, do some traveling, and talk to interesting people, they are bound to come up with clever ideas for stories, inventions, games, products, recipes, and businesses. However, that's as far as most folks go. They think of the ideas, but they never engage in the experimentation, development, revision, and production required to make the ideas become tangible realities.

At first, this used to annoy me. I remember what would happen after I co-wrote the novel *The Gift* with Holly G. Miller. The story was about a man who could transfuse time from one person to another. I would be at a bookstore or a writers conference autographing copies of the book, and at least a dozen people would say to me, "I had this idea before you did. I came up with this plot years ago. I already thought up this whole story when I was in high school/college/the navy/prison."

I was tempted to say, "Well, if you're so much smarter than I am, how come I've got this novel out and you're in line to pay money to me for *your* story?" But I held my tongue, because it dawned on me that, yeah, maybe some of them did come up with a similar idea. Totally possible. But, who cares? These people didn't spend weeks upon weeks dreaming up the specific elements of the story that would make it work (characters, settings, plot tension, subplot interaction, boffo closing), and they didn't spend six months pounding out the rough draft of the fifteen chapters, and they didn't spend another four months rewriting the first draft and then selling it to a publisher.

## What if I'm Not Feeling Creative?

Ideas are a dime a dozen. Published, successful books are rare. It takes work, real work. My literary hero, Jack London, once said, "Don't loaf and invite inspiration; light out after it with a club, and if you don't get it you will nonetheless get something that looks remarkably like it."

This advice comes from the man who was the first person ever to earn a million dollars strictly from professional writing. Jack wrote one thousand words per day, whether it took him just an hour or it took all day. He was dedicated to his craft and thoroughly disciplined. Though he died in 1916, he is still my role model. I keep a poster of him in my office. He lived the phrase "just do it" long before Nike came along.

I've seen copies of his manuscripts in the Henry Huntington Library in California. I've seen where he wrote one thousand words one day, then came back the next day with a different color ink and edited the previous day's work and then went on to write a new one thousand words.

No one would say Jack London wasn't creative. However, *The Call of the Wild* and *White Fang* and "To Build a Fire" didn't write themselves. Between the ages of twenty-two and forty, London produced 190 published short stories and twenty-six novels. He was living proof that creative ideas aren't hard to come by, but finishing manuscripts takes real dedication.

So, do you want to be more creative? Okay, begin by keeping that wonderful mind of yours open to all those great ideas flowing through it, but then carve out the time to get those ideas down on paper.

### *Creative* Writer Tip 2
### Vaporize writers Block
### with Creative-Thinking
### Breakthroughs

**The ability to** place a common object in a new environment can lead to creative breakthroughs in business, writing, commerce, science, and education. Let me prove the point by giving you a simple but powerful example.

Text messaging is now the rage. However, it has existed for nearly two centuries. Prior to cell phones and iPads, it was done on postcards. People would use from 140 to 160 characters (numbers or letters) to tell family and friends about having arrived at a destination safely, what the weather was like, what the most enjoyable event had been thus far, and what the next day's outing would be. Writers had to be concise, focused, and clever (such as saving space by ending with *C U soon, luv, Tina*). Modern text messaging is nothing more than postcard-writing on a miniature screen.

When writers complain about writer's block, often they are actually saying that they're confining and restricting their range of creativity by staying within fixed modes of thinking. Said another way, they can visualize only a postcard made of paper, written upon with an ink pen, and dispatched by placing a stamp on it and mailing it. They cannot envision a postcard as a small screen with a keypad and electronic-transfer capability. They are "blocked" by conventionality.

## Tap into Divergent and Convergent Thinking

In professional writing there are two traditional avenues of thinking:

*Divergent thinking* (often referred to as brainstorming) is the "anything goes" aspect of creative writing. An individual author—or a team of ad copywriters or TV sitcom writers—will try to come up with as many ideas as possible for a storyline, in as many different genres as possible, in as many new presentation styles as possible. Thus, a basic love story might go through experimental modes of being a comedy and then a tragedy, being set in a modern venue but later changed to a historical locale, or being drafted as a screenplay but later getting transformed into a novel. At this initial stage it is all about experimentation, vastness, and distinctiveness.

*Convergent thinking* (often referred to as aligning and editing) must then bring order out of chaos. By requiring the writer to sift through the melee of material, the process turns the creative writer into a focused proofreader and organized editor. The eventual formation of an outline and summary results from discarding the useless, refining the cumbersome, redirecting the misdirected, and sharpening the dull.

However, divergent-to-convergent path of thinking is not as innovative as it purports to be. New stimuli are needed to make the two thinking processes more radical, more vibrant, and more dynamic. Such stimuli are often avoided, however, because they seem bizarre, unrealistic, or even dangerous.

## Consider Remote Viewing as a Stimulus-for-Thought Process

One way to experience a creative-thinking breakthrough can be seen in the fascinating study of remote viewing. In the late 1970s, the United States military discovered that certain individuals had developed a mental discipline so rigid and concentrated, they could actually imagine activities going on elsewhere in the world. Such activities later proved to be virtually what truly was happening in that locale at that very time.

Here's how it was done. One person would be given the task of immersing himself into the life of, say, a foreign dictator—the dictator's family history, his education, his eating habits, his manner of dress, his way of talking, the home he lived in, the car he drove, the weekly schedule he followed. Sometimes the analyst would spend hours watching movies and film clips of this dictator. Other times he would listen for many days to the dictator's speeches and then spend other days reading his letters, college papers, journal entries, and e-mails.

Before long, the person studying the dictator vicariously stepped into the alternate persona of becoming that person. At that stage, he could close his eyes, relax in a chair or lie on the floor, and someone could say, "The dictator is going to a political rally today. Tell us what is happening." At that point, the alternate persona would concentrate on becoming the dictator and would undergo an experience known as "bilocation." Although he was physically in a room at an army base in the United States, he also was consciously in another country simultaneously "seeing" the activities of the dictator in question. And, remarkably, these bilocation experiences were stunningly accurate, as was proved later. This helped the military learn to anticipate sneak attacks, planned embargoes, secret treaties, and covert espionage activities by its enemies.

Who is to say that writers could not use this same process during the convergent phase of creative writing? After having spent a substantial amount of time brainstorming about a story's central character and all the trappings that go with him or her, why couldn't a writer just step into that person's life and become him or her? The novel or short story could unfold through self-interviewing by saying, "The school teacher is going to the board meeting tonight. Talk about what is happening with that." Let an audio recorder capture all the information. Later, transcribe those descriptions, passages of dialogue, and outcomes.

## Innovation versus Adaptation

Generally speaking, creative thinkers—inventors, fiction writers, artists, composers, mathematicians—make radical breakthroughs and devise totally original concepts. They are known as innovative thinkers. Others, known as adaptive thinkers, see ways to refine and improve existing concepts. Writers can benefit from knowing how both of these types of individuals go about solving problems.

Very few people are true innovative thinkers. And, unfortunately, these individuals are usually ridiculed as liars or, worse, labeled insane. Copernicus was actually arrested when he announced that the sun, not the earth, was the center of the solar system. Columbus couldn't get funding in his native Italy when he wanted to prove, by sailing west, that the world was round, not flat. Einstein was called a quack when he presented an alternative view to Newtonian physics. Dr. Christiaan Barnard was called "Frankenstein" when he proposed the idea of transplanting a baboon heart into the body of a man.

Each of these radical thinkers demonstrates lessons we can apply to the craft of writing.

You have to be an expert about everything in your field before you can discover something missing from it.

You have to be willing to believe in your idea, even when naysayers abound.

You have to allow your audience to "catch up" to you and your ideas, even though it may take decades.

Thus, when Samuel Beckett wrote "Waiting for Godot" and initiated Theatre of the Absurd, he lacked an audience during much of his lifetime. However, today dozens of college and civic theatre groups produce the play annually, and it has run on Broadway with star performers such as Steve Martin and Robin Williams. Similarly, when television scriptwriters conceived the idea of "reality shows," in which the "actors" were real people facing real dilemmas without scripts or rehearsals or retakes, network executives thought it was the stupidest thing they ever heard of. Finally, however, one sponsor agreed to underwrite a trial show called *Survivor*, and it became a blockbuster hit for ten years. It led to dozens upon dozens of clone reality TV shows. So, innovative writing can still be done, rare though it may be.

## Presenting Stories in Fresh Ways

Creative advancements often come through modifications of something already in existence. When Henry Ford took Eli Whitney's original idea of assembly-line gun manufacturing and modified it as a way of turning out Model T and Model A cars at the rate of one every five minutes, he was just improving on an existing idea. Likewise, when Ford's competitors later starting producing cars that were green or blue or white or red instead of Ford's basic black color, they out-innovated Ford and took his markets away from him.

Writers have done similar things for centuries. Dante's "The New Life" was expanded to Chaucer's "Troilus and Cressida," which was modified into Shakespeare's "Romeo and Juliet," which became Bernstein's musical "West Side Story." Same tale, just new venues. Other times the identical story was simply revamped, as in the endless ways Dickens's *A Christmas Carol* has been retold as stage plays, dramatically acted and animated movies, comic books, puppet shows, video games, TV specials, and even parodies, e.g., *Scrooged* with Bill Murray. Oddly enough, audiences never seem to tire of being told the same story as long as it is presented in a fresh way.

What all of this information tells us is that writer's block is more about limited thinking ability than it is limited writing skills.

Writers need to call upon the full range of thinking models: (a) being unconventional enough to see the postcard as a screen; (b) being both divergent and convergent but injecting new stimuli to expand the procedures; and (c) being innovative or adaptive, per the needs of each writing challenge. The answers are all there, in your head. You just need better ways of digging them out.

---

## *Creative* Writer Tip 3
## Jumpstarts I Learned
## Accidentally at Writers
## Conferences

**If you teach** at as many writers conferences as I do, you learn a few things by osmosis. Let me share some examples with you. The first one has to do with using both hemispheres of our brain to boost creativity.

Back when Tom Clark was editor of *Writer's Digest*, he and I were on the faculty of a writers conference at the Ridgecrest Conference Center in North Carolina. The director had created an elaborate murder mystery as entertainment for the faculty and registrants, and she had divided us into two-person investigative units.

Tom and I were teamed as a kind of Joe-and-Frank *Dragnet* partnership. Since Tom had a more extensive background in investigative journalism than I, we weren't as much of a good cop/bad cop team as we were a good cop/dumb cop team. But I tried to hold my own.

Tom and I looked at the scene of the crime. We questioned the witnesses and the officers who were first on the scene (all played by retreat-center personnel). We then questioned the next of kin, the hired help, and the victim's coworkers. In only about thirty minutes, Tom and I had discerned who the killer was and why and how she had committed the murder. Most of the other teams either gave up after a couple of hours, or they arrived at the wrong conclusions.

## Right-brain/Left-brain Epiphany

Interestingly enough, that game led me to an epiphany. When I thought back to how Tom and I had cracked the case, it dawned on me that we had approached the solution from different perspectives, but we had combined our unique insights.

Tom kept hammering home pragmatic questions about details: "Where was the body found? Who were the victim's known enemies? What sort of poison was used to kill the victim?" I, on the other hand, kept in mind that this was a game. Thus, I kept pondering such things as, "If I wanted to surprise the participants completely, how would I add a twist to what is going on here?" and "If I were writing this as a mystery, which of these so-called clues would I insert as red herrings or blind alleys or false leads?"

I think this was much like right-brain and left-brain activity. As writers, we need to be dreamers and speculators and what-if imagineers, but then we must anchor our fantasies with realistic circumstances, logical proceedings, and believable characters. (Not *just* the facts, ma'am, but certainly *some* of the facts.)

## Imagining Dialogue

One time I was teaching at a four-day conference in Montreal, Quebec. Due to an electrical storm, several American television networks were temporarily knocked out. Most of what was left to watch at night was a series of programs in which everyone spoke French. I don't speak French except for *marquee*, *résumé*, and *oo-la-la*.

For fun, I turned down the volume and started adlibbing the shows, pretending I was a translator but making up my own dialogue based on the characters' behavior, expressions, clothing, props, and emotions. Crazy as it may sound, I started coming up with some incredibly good storylines. As to whether they had anything to do with what was actually being played out on the TV show, I still have no clue. It didn't matter. I had stumbled on an atypical writing exercise in which to generate original storylines.

## Put Your Characters into Improv

I once spoke at a writers conference that featured an entertainment night. The festivities included a segment where audience members were pulled up on stage and dropped into an improvisation scene. I got recruited. I was handed a note card that said, "You are selling magazine subscriptions door to door. Try to close a sale." I was not allowed to explain to anyone else on stage what my note card said. I just had to start acting my part. The other four character-assignments were a cop on a beat, a senile old lady who'd lost her way, a dogcatcher in search of a stray mutt, and a robot.

The five of us were videotaped. Viewing the tape later, I was amazed at how smoothly all of us eased into our roles and created humor by way of pratfalls and jokes and adlibs and funny faces. We actually pulled together a silly yet somewhat feasible storyline.

Subsequently, I would often begin writing my novels by jotting short descriptions of six or eight characters on note cards and then jumbling the cards together, forcing myself to find out what these people would do if they were put on stage together. Invariably, it led to some clever plot concepts.

## Create the Physical Scene First

On opening night at a writers conference in Houston, the director created an icebreaker exercise to get everyone in the mood for fun. She passed out pieces of candy to everyone. She gave flashlights to ten people. She handed a long, thin sheet of aluminum to two men, and stationed one man at each end. She set up three large fans and assigned control of the switches to three people. Then, like an orchestra conductor, she said, "Let's create a cliché, folks. It was a dark and stormy night!"

She directed us to remove the crinkly wrappers from our pieces of hard candy and then squeeze and roll the cellophane with our fingers. All eighty-five people doing that produced the sound of rain. Then she signaled for one of the fans to start. This was followed by having people turn flashlights on and off at four-second intervals. Next, she had the men whip the piece of aluminum, and it sounded like thunder. Finally, she cued the other two fans to kick in. She told us all to keep doing our parts, but to close our eyes. I swear, it actually did sound and feel like a dark and stormy night, yet we were all indoors at a motel conference room.

In creating scenes for my short stories, stage plays, or novels, I have used this mood-enhancing trick. For example, when I was getting ready to write a scene for one of my novels that was to take place in the Smoky Mountains, I started playing a tape of woodland sounds, I sprayed my office with pine-scented air freshener, and I rubbed some tree bark between my hands. I closed my eyes, and I was there. The scene was vivid to me; thus, I was able to make it vivid to my readers.

So, take my advice. The next time you are at a writers conference and the director wants to play a silly game or engage in some role playing, be willing to participate. You might accidentally learn something of value.

**When I teach** fiction, I tell my students to look at their lives as data banks of plot ideas. All lives contain human dramas. Some dramatic moments are good—such as being announced the class valedictorian—others are bad, like being fired from your job. The novelist's challenge is to raise routine human events to levels of entertainment by increasing their dramatic tension, by retelling them with humor, or by having them teach some sort of lesson. Novels show life in an abridged format where the emphasis is on the emotional rather than the factual aspects of events.

To help stimulate your memory in your search for plot ideas inspired by your personal life, pull out family albums and look at the way you've celebrated birthdays and holidays. Watch home movies or videos; talk to your older relatives about their lives; read your grade-school diaries and journals; go up to the attic and search through the treasury of forgotten toys, school yearbooks, and outdated clothes.

As episodes from your earlier years become vivid again, take notes. Try to figure out ways to enhance the real stories in order to make them fascinating enough for fiction. For example, remind yourself of the fear you felt bringing home that fifth-grade report card with the two Ds on it. Now, ask yourself how that scene could be made even more intense if you wrote it as a work of fiction. Maybe the two Ds would keep the main character off the basketball team or the cheerleading squad; or perhaps the Ds would result in punishment of no TV, MP3, iPad, or video use for six weeks, along with no allowance. What else could those bad grades do to ruin a fifth-grader's life?

## Blending Your Sources for Novel Inspiration

After you have spent a couple of hours jotting down memories and plot ideas, organize your material. Put each scene into its proper chronological position amidst all your other scenes. Go back and amplify each episode by adding more notes about what led up to the event, what motivated you to do what you did, how you felt about the circumstances, and what the long-range ramifications were of the actions you took.

Next, judge your material. If any particular episode doesn't seem real, determine how you can write it in such a way as to give it credibility. Come up with ways in which an event of the past can still be relevant to today's readers. Eliminate any sappy or overly melodramatic anecdotes. Create elements of suspense that will make the reader continue turning pages.

Always keep in mind that no writer creates out of a void. All writers must draw ideas from what they have read or heard or experienced firsthand. What makes this limitless in its range of creativity, however, is that all three methods may be blended. You can take an event from your own life, modify it by adding characters you have read about, and then conclude with an anecdote someone else told you last week.

When you get finished, the completed novel may seem to have no direct relationship to your personal life at all, but in a very real sense, it does, indeed. However, only you, as the novelist, will know just how much.

Any writer who has ever stared at a blank screen or sheet of paper, unable to come up with a story idea, knows the feeling of being creatively comatose. Try as you may, nothing comes to mind.

If that is ever you, don't blow your brain out in frustration. Instead, feed it new ideas and have some laughs along the way. Here is an idea from childhood that will help you put the creativity back into creative writing.

As a youngster, you may have had a fold-over book that was divided into three sections. For example, the first scene shows a normal-looking man. Then you flip over a new top third section, and the man is wearing a pirate hat, has an eye patch, and a parrot sits on his shoulder. You then flip over a new bottom third, and the man is dressed in policeman's trousers with handcuffs, a billy club, and a pistol hanging from his belt.

## Rev Your Imagination

Creative writers can play a mental version of this game. Imagine a business executive in a suit and holding a briefcase. Now, flip a new bottom section on him, and suddenly he's wearing jogging shorts. Why? Well, maybe it's because he's actually a model on his way to a photo shoot for men's sports gear. Or he's an avid jogger who runs every day during lunch hour. Or he's a bachelor and is so far behind on his laundry, he wore jogging shorts under his suit. Jot down all those ideas.

Now flip over the top section. Suddenly he's wearing the upturned collar of a clergyman, has a neatly trimmed gray beard, and is wearing wire-rimmed glasses. Why? Well, maybe he's a reservist with the army and serves part-time as a chaplain, or he's a seminary professor who teaches ancient languages. Or perhaps he's a con artist who travels from city to city posing as an evangelist. Write down all those ideas.

Now flip the middle section. Whoa! Look! Now he has on a brightly colored vest with a watch chain extended from one side pocket to the other. Why? Maybe he's a riverboat gambler or a circus sideshow barker. Or perhaps he sings in a barbershop quartet. Add these new options to your list of notes.

Pause a moment, and in your mind's eye, look at this silly person your mental flip-book has created. How could one person ever combine such diverse appearances and occupations? Ridiculous! Funny! Silly! Unbelievable! Or is it?

## Build Your Character's Dossier

Start to play detective. How might all these elements be combined to form a dossier on this man? Hmmm. Perhaps he's a youth minister (upturned collar) who works at a church camp (jogging shorts) and whose hobby is singing in an old-fashioned gospel music group (vest). Or perhaps he's a hospital chaplain (upturned collar) who assists disabled children with their physical therapy regimens (gym shorts) but who is also ready to help raise funds for the new hospital wing by being part of a vaudeville night benefit show (fancy vest).

Let your imagination run wild. Have fun. Come up with several different profiles for this character. If it is hard for you to do this exercise in your imagination, create a real flip-book. Gather magazines and catalogs and clip photos of chefs, pilots, mechanics, parachutists, barbers, cowboys, and firefighters to stimulate your thinking.

Once you've developed one set of profiles for your lead character, run through the process two or three more times—for a villain, a sweetheart, and maybe even a sidekick. Then start imagining how the various characters might come head to head in a conflict strong enough to evolve into a plot.

For example, could the aforementioned chaplain face an ethical challenge when, in privileged communication, the director of the hospital fundraiser tells him he has stolen some of the show's earnings? Uh-oh, what does the chaplain do now?

All sorts of mix-and-match scenarios are possible. Keep on playing with the flip-book until you've matched the right characters with the right plot conflict.

When that happens…you'll just "flip"!

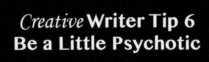

**Creative Writer Tip 6
Be a Little Psychotic**

**First, let me** emphasize vigorously that I am *not* in favor of anyone using so-called "recreational drugs." I abhor the use of LSD, marijuana, heroin, cocaine, or even alcohol. That's just how square I truly am. And second, what I'm about to teach you may have initially been stimulated by drugs, but it can be achieved without their use. That is what this tip is about.

Here's what happened. Some years ago on a March morning I slipped on concrete during a thunderstorm. I fell and cracked my pelvic socket and wound up in a hospital where I was given morphine, aspirin, and Vicodin to help curb the incredible pain I was experiencing. For a person like me who never uses drugs, this pain-relieving "cocktail" sent me into orbit. For about six hours, my memories, dreams, fears, anxieties, imaginings, and real-time events merged, overlapped, bled into each other, morphed, and combined into bizarre new configurations. And, amazingly, when the drugs wore off, I had vivid recollections of many of these wacky experiences. I got a tape recorder and saved them before they got away.

## Literary Precedence

There is literary precedence for creating plots by pushing the mind into innovative experiences that are far beyond the norm. Samuel Coleridge claimed that his partial poem "Kubla Khan" came to him in a dream. Marcel Proust made his brain move faster than his writing pen when developing stream of conscious writing for his novel *Swann's Way.* Lewis Carroll overlapped exaggeration, satire, and hallucination in creating the maniacal world of *Alice in Wonderland.* G. K. Chesterton's surreal novel *The Man Who Was Thursday* literally carried the subtitle, *A Nightmare.* To the best of my knowledge, none of these writers made use of narcotics for creative stimulation. However, it is obvious they were able to force the mind to think in new dimensions and to escape normal restrictions.

In my case, the drugs in my system caused me to imagine that the MRI machine I was placed inside was a bunker, and I was back in Vietnam as a twenty-two-year-old kid fighting the war again. I should explain: an MRI machine emits a rat-a-tat-tat sound very similar to an M-60 machine gun. Mixed with this was a sensation that I was an escape artist who'd been locked in a trunk (the MRI cylinder) and placed under the Detroit River, no doubt brought on by the fact that three days before the accident, I had been reading an article about Harry Houdini. But thrown into the mix was also my secret hope that I had never really been injured and that I was back in my college classroom rapping on my podium, bringing my class to order, ready to give a lecture. The MRI enclosure, the exam-room noises, and the medicinal odors were sending my drug-induced imagination in myriad directions.

From this hodgepodge of sensory infusions, I later came up with a short story about a tunnel rat in Vietnam who escaped pursuit of the enemy and later stood before a class to teach his techniques of tunneling to other soldiers. Additionally, subsequent dream-and-reality collisions led to ideas for other short stories, one play, and the subplot of a novel. This experience convinced me that purposeful dream hemorrhaging could expand the arenas of creativity and tap into the reservoirs of personal experience most of us never recognize as having useful story content. Here now is how to do it sans drugs.

## The Power of the Mind to Create Solutions

For a long time psychologists have known that one way to use the subconscious mind for problem-solving is to feed it a problem before going to sleep. For example, by writing out in longhand what a problem is, then reading it the last thing before going to sleep and the first thing upon awakening, the problem will be implanted into the subconscious, where it will be examined, studied, and eventually solved.

This method can be amplified for creative writers. Here are two techniques you can try:

Consider a plot difficulty, such as how to get two characters to fall in love. Write that down. However, along with that add the *era* you want the characters to be in (the Roaring Twenties? World War II? the twenty-first century?); add the *genre* you want the story to be presented in (romance? Western? mystery?); and add the *format* you wish to write the story in (novel? movie script? epic poem?). Keep your notepad or audio recorder near you throughout the day, and make a record of any and all ideas that come to mind related to your plot's problem.

Another method involves sensory mix-and-match. For example, put two radically different scents in your nose, one at a time, and then simultaneously. Sniff mustard and licorice. What does that do to your memory? Sniff roses and shoe polish...potting soil and turpentine...fish oil and a pine bough. Your mind will have to struggle to assimilate these conflicting aromas, odors, and smells. That mental struggle will send you into new thought combinations. Hey, maybe the roses and shoe polish will lead to a story about a first date, in which a young man is buffing his shoes while keeping the bouquet for his sweetheart close at hand. Let your imagination run with it.

Yet another process involves interpretive superimposing. Take three very similar stories and read them in interrupted patterns. For example, get copies of "Troilus and Cressida," "Romeo and Juliet," and "West Side Story." Read the first ten pages of one, then ten pages of the next, and then ten pages of the third. Repeat the process as you move to the next ten pages. Repeat it again…and again. How are these works absolutely identical? How are they radically different? What is predictable in each one? What is a complete surprise in each one? Where are the timeless themes, and where are the new messages? Compare and contrast them until aspects of all three re-form as something totally your own—missed plot opportunities in the originals…new character arcs in response to different challenges…vibrant new settings. Such overlapping reading won't confuse the mind so much as it will enrich it with burgeoning plot options.

A fourth technique involves storyboard shuffling. This requires the brain to see visual images while combining unrelated storylines. The object is to make the imagination come up with something logical from something disorganized. For example, go online or visit the library and make photocopies of bygone-era newspapers' dramatic comic strips (*Mary Worth, Rex Morgan, M.D., Terry and the Pirates, Dick Tracy, Prince Valiant, Little Orphan Annie*). Cut out the individual comic-strip boxes, mix them randomly, and align them in new sequences.

Why is physician Rex Morgan now rushing to assist detective Dick Tracy in bringing senior citizen Mary Worth to the orphanage where little Annie is being abused? Let your imagination run rampant with these convoluted, wild, emotionally charged plots. Speculate, question, examine, and wonder, all the while taking notes.

These methods are not routine. They will probably be out of your comfort zone, and they may even give you a headache. If so, it'll mean you're using synapses that have not joined forces previously. That'll be progress. Writers need to move beyond the norm, the dull, the bland. It's true enough that writers are dream-weavers. But if the patterns of the dreams are as regulated as a cross-stitch outline, the surprises will be missing, and the magic will not be baffling.

Don't be afraid to be a little psychotic. A bit of mental bloodletting can be the cure to your creative coagulation.

# Chapter 5
# The Nitty-Gritty of Fiction

**Nitty-Gritty Tip 1**
**Writing Micro Fiction**

**I've never found** writing short fiction to be easy. Developing a plot, establishing a setting, creating believable characters, infusing realistic dialogue, and presenting a logical resolution to the story's crisis—all within 2,000 to 5,000 words—is a challenge. But if that's bad, an even greater challenge is trying to write the "micro" short story (750 to 1,250 words), currently popular in literary digests, church take-home papers, and regional periodicals. The popularity of flash fiction—stories fewer than 1,000 words—has caught on big time now. Many periodicals that specialize in flash fiction, such as *Havok* and *Splickety*, publish each issue in print and online editions.

My first micro was called "Could Beethoven Have Made It in Nashville?" (*Stereo*, Spring 1973). It was a one-thousand-word comedy with a simple premise: if Ludwig van Beethoven were alive today and tried to get a job as a musician in Nashville, Tennessee, would anyone hire him?

What made the story work was its simplicity. There was one setting (a country music recording studio), only two characters (Beethoven and the studio engineer), and one basic joke (a talented man is out of his element). The comedy came from the fact that Beethoven had long hair like modern musicians, and he wore long, black coattails like Johnny Cash. He looked the part. Yet, he couldn't deliver the goods. The comedic format was structured around the dialogue between the two men, both talented artists but neither one having a clue as to what the other one was talking about. Very little author narrative was required.

The micro story is wedged inside very strict framing. The setting usually is limited to one spot (a classroom, a library alcove, the backseat of a taxi). Walk-on characters may be needed, but the central characters are usually limited to just two people (dad with son, boss and new employee, doctor seeing patient). The plot must be confined to one problem or crisis that can be resolved without extenuating circumstances or plot complications.

Writing micro fiction is like playing with a toy telescope. If you look into the small aperture, you see a wide panorama of distant scenes brought into close view (the novel, the traditional short story). However, if you turn the telescope around and look into the wide aperture, you see very small images and a very limited field of vision (the micro story).

Ideas for micro plots are often derived from scenes or snatches of conversation or real life lessons that are heard or witnessed on the run. The idea for my 950-word story "The Competition" (*Challenge*, Feb. 15, 1976) came from two overlapping events at my church.

Our custodian had retired that year. At his farewell dinner, he said that in his youth he had planned to be a preacher. He received a scholarship to a Bible college but then broke his hip in a farm accident. He had to forfeit the scholarship and remain bedridden. He felt it was the worst thing that could ever have happened to him. However, he fell in love with the nurse who came by to check on him each afternoon.

They married, raised a family, and had a marvelous life together. He said his accident turned out to be the best "break" he'd ever had.

About this same time, our church sponsored a statewide youth-talent rally, with prizes ranging from savings bonds to college scholarships. A young trumpet player from our church took second place in the instrumental performance category. He was devastated. Someone else received the scholarship he so desperately wanted. I heard him say, "This is the worst thing that could ever have happened to me"…and, with that, I had the basis of my micro story.

I opened the story at the competition with the old custodian wishing the young musician good luck. The boy then performed well but finished second. He couldn't face his friends or family, so he retreated to the church basement.

The old man followed him, told him his own "worse thing ever" story and how it became his "best thing ever" story. They took a moment to pray together for the boy to have a right attitude toward competition. The story ended with the old man reminding the boy that he was only a junior and he still had next year in which to compete for a scholarship. The boy lifted the trumpet, gave it a practice toot, and the story was over.

Again, we see one setting (a church), two characters (the boy and the custodian) and one plot lesson (learning to see defeat in a broader context). This micro story must be that concise. Its dialogue must be crisp, to the point, and always provide necessary information or move the plot forward. Adjectives and adverbs must be eliminated through the use of visual nouns (*mansion* or *shack* rather than *house*) and action verbs (*slapped* or *tapped* rather than *touched*). The plot conflict must be created at the onset of the story. The ending must evoke a reader response (a laugh, a nod of agreement, a wince of surprise).

Although I find short fiction very challenging, I continue to write it. It is the best practice I know for learning how to make each word count. That discipline carries over into everything else I write. The scenes in my novels are more plot intensive if I think in a micro mentality. The dialogue in my interviews is more distilled and pertinent if I think micro. Even my feature reporting is better if I think in micro—keep to the facts, limit the scope, get to the crux of the problem immediately, and don't leave the reader baffled at the end.

And…that's the short of it, friends!

# Nitty-Gritty Tip 2
# The Parameters of
# Violence in Fiction

**While doing the** required reading to earn MA and PhD degrees in English, I was amazed at how often in classic literature scenes of violence occurred "off stage." *Hamlet* contains the line, "Rosencrantz and Guildenstern are dead." Yeah, sure, we know Hamlet has set them up, but we are never allowed to witness their actual assassinations. We are just told that the boys are goners. It's rather anticlimactic after so much foreshadowing.

An even more bizarre off-stage incident occurs in *Clarissa* by Samuel Richardson. Poor, dear Clarissa frets for hundreds of pages that she will be cornered and raped by a male adversary. In letter after letter, she bemoans the fact that she is utterly vulnerable. Then, in one letter, she writes to a friend, "The deed is done." That's the whole rape scene. Now, I'm not a sadist, but, come on, after two hundred fifty pages of build up, I had expected some face clawing, piercing screams, and flailing of arms and legs. Instead, we get, "The deed is done." Huh?

## Fill in the Blanks

There are times when off-stage violence can be more tasteful than eyewitness observation. I don't want to watch Oedipus gouge out his eyes. I don't need to observe the surgeons amputate Lieutenant Dan's legs after Forrest Gump rescues him. And I'd rather not watch as Hannibal Lecter removes the facial skin of a police guard. For a fact, these off-stage scenes act as pivots to what then become major new directions for the plots. Oedipus appears in two more plays as a blind man. Lieutenant Dan becomes ten times more compelling as a disabled civilian than he was as an army officer. Lecter on the loose becomes far more terrifying than Lecter in prison.

Sidney Sheldon used to say that the sexiest scenes in his novels were the ones in which he gave the readers the set-up and then let them fill in the blanks. In fact, he sometimes received criticism for being too lewd and graphic, when, in reality, he had only made allusions and inferences and had let the readers take things as far as they chose. Likewise, I think the same can be said for violence. The shower scene in *Psycho* never shows a blade touch skin, yet it is more chilling than most of the blood-and-gore scenes in modern slasher movies.

Violence has a place in drama. To avoid it entirely is idealizing and ridiculous. When my son was young, I used to watch *G.I. Joe* cartoons with him. The Joes would fire a million laser rounds at the Cobra enemy army, yet never hit anyone. Similarly, the Cobra army would return a million shots against the Joes, yet they never shot a single man. These were supposed to be the two most elite fighting forces on the planet, yet they were the worst shots in history. It was ludicrous. And don't even get me started on how *The A-Team* spent five seasons blowing up cars, trucks, airplanes, warehouses, and bad-guy hideouts, yet every villain always got up, dusted himself off, and walked away. (The movie version of the TV show was more realistic... at least in this one respect.)

## Justifiable Violence

There are times when avoiding violence in a scene just doesn't ring true. Even Jesus upset the tables of the moneychangers and gave a vitriolic tongue-lashing to those found in the "den of thieves." The challenge is to make such scenes align with the nature of the person taking the action and be believable within the context of the scene being presented.

A brilliant example of this is found in the 1956 movie *Friendly Persuasion*. A Quaker farmer in southern Indiana (Gary Cooper as Jess Birdwell) is trying to stay neutral during the Civil War and thus keep himself and his sons from having to engage in violence of any kind. However, while Jess Birdwell is out on his land one day, a Confederate soldier shoots at him, and the bullet grazes the farmer's forehead, knocking him down. He pretends to be dead, hoping the soldier will go away. Instead, the Reb advances on Birdwell to finish him off.

In an act of self-preservation, Birdwell jumps up. Catching the soldier off guard, he grabs the man's rifle and pins him against a tree with it. The two men lock in mortal combat until Birdwell succeeds in wresting the rifle away from the soldier. He points the barrel directly at the Confederate trooper. The soldier is horrified, thinking surely he will be shot at pointblank range by this civilian he has tried to kill.

For a moment we see the rage in Birdwell's eyes. The soldier has already shot him in the head and fought him hand to hand. Birdwell has every right, in self-defense, to kill the man. However, Birdwell's Quaker beliefs slowly begin to resurface, and we see a narrowing of his eyes and the forming of a grim expression. He jerks the barrel of the weapon in sideways motions, signaling for the soldier to go away, to get off his land. The man is dumbfounded, but he staggers away. Then, in a moment of outrage, Birdwell grabs the rifle by the barrel and swings it viciously against the trunk of the tree, over and over, until the weapon cracks, breaks, and shatters.

This scene works. The fistfight is believable, even though it involves a Quaker. The threat with the gun is believable, even though done by a Quaker. And the release of pent-up anger and rage as evidenced by the savage smashing of the rifle against the tree is totally believable because—Quaker or not—Birdwell is a normal human being with fight-or-flight preservation instincts. Personally, if a scene can be labeled "tasteful, appropriate violence," this scene, in my opinion, certainly qualifies.

## The Parameters

What we are left with then is an understanding that although violence is offensive to most readers, they nevertheless understand that all people have the potential to unleash it if sufficiently provoked. And therein lies the secret of making it work in fiction. If a scene of violence makes the reader say, "I can see myself doing that under those circumstances," then it is not only realistic, but it is also acceptable, honest, and justifiable.

Just don't go overboard with violence, because if you do, your editor will have to put the ear back on the victim—as Jesus did after Peter went on a sword-slashing spree—and ask for a rewrite. Keep it in bounds.

# Nitty-Gritty Tip 3
## Suspending Disbelief

**In the mid-1960s** an episode of *Candid Camera* went tragically wrong. Alan Funt entered a kindergarten class and spent time talking one-on-one with five-year-olds, asking about their favorite toys, best friends, and family pets. All the children were talkative, animated, and friendly. Then another adult came in and led the child into a different room for a couple of minutes, during which time Alan Funt hid behind a curtain and a two-foot dummy looking exactly like him was put in the chair in his place.

Each child was then led back in as a hidden camera was filming him or her. The adults wanted to see if the children would look at the dummy of Alan Funt and then just start talking to it as though it were the same person. However, in each of four tries, the children became horrified, started screaming in panic, and tried to escape the room, fully believing that the dummy *was* Alan Funt, only now horribly disfigured.

A follow-up to this experience turned out to be amazing. Children were brought in one at a time and introduced to a ventriloquist who had a dummy sitting on his lap. The children were interviewed by both the man and by the dummy. This time the children treated the dummy as if it were a real human being. They answered his questions, laughed with him, and even shook hands with him. As long as the dummy was an identifiable entity in and of itself, and it stayed in character, the children had no problem with it whatsoever.

I was an adult when I saw this *Candid Camera* broadcast, but I had no difficulty believing its veracity. You see, as a child my favorite show after school every day was *Howdy Doody*. I loved that show and its iconic string-puppet star. I never missed an episode. In my childlike mind, Howdy was as real as fellow cast members Buffalo Bob, Clarabell the Clown, and Chief Thunderthud. In fact, when I was eleven and they announced the show was going off the air, I was depressed for weeks. (Years later, my wife told me that when she heard the announcement as a girl, she cried the whole day.)

If you had pressed me as a kid, yeah, I probably would have said Howdy was a puppet, but I never processed that mentally. I was having too much fun accepting Howdy as a walking, talking, adventure-loving, yodeling boy. Likewise for Dilly Dally, Phineas T. Bluster, and Flub-a-Dub. Because they had emotions, personalities, dreams, fears, and a sense of humor, I related to them, liked them, and bonded with them, marionettes or not.

## The Rules of Make-Believe

As fiction writers, we can draw many lessons from this childhood openness to parallel worlds, fantasy situations, and make-believe characters. Human nature is bent toward a love of escapism and altered realities, and the reasons for this are probably myriad. Escapism tickles our imagination; it provides a haven for us that is safer than the real world; it gives us friends who won't let us down; it allows us vicariously to be part of heroic deeds. Shoot, I'm no psychiatrist, but who needs a degree to see what is blatant: *People like to suspend disbelief.*

This does not mean, however, that anything goes. In writing novels, short stories, stage plays, and musicals, I've learned that my audiences will follow me as long as I don't burst the bubble of disbelief. To that end, some rules must be followed.

First, ***characters must be consistent.*** The mistake Alan Funt made was that he introduced one character (a human adult) and then instantly morphed it into a dissimilar character (a dummy). That was illogical, unfair, and irrational, and that same rule applies to fiction writing. Superman can *pretend* to be Clark Kent, as long as we know that underneath he's still "the man of steel." The Pevensie children can go through the wardrobe and enter Narnia, as long as they remain the same persons they were upon entering. Ditto for Alice when she falls into Wonderland, King Kong when he's brought to New York, and Phileas Fogg as he travels around the world in eighty days. The consistency of a character allows us, as readers, to place ourselves into this character's circumstances, identifying with the struggles of facing great challenges.

Now this is not to say that characters cannot evolve. Certainly, Peter Parker slowly, steadily, painfully moves into his role as Spider-Man, but it takes a long period of time. Likewise, Tarzan can eventually learn to speak English, wear clothes, and eat with utensils. We accept all this as readers because we, too, evolve over time. We can learn to speak French, but it will take years. We can lose weight, but only after dieting and exercising for many months. Here's the key in all this: Characters must be consistent unto themselves to the point that readers can see them, accept them, and relate to them.

Second, ***morals, behavior patterns, and motivating factors must be human-like.*** Many fictional characters are not human. Among my favorites are the *Velveteen Rabbit*, Frodo, Chewbacca, Elmer Fudd, and the little robot Wall-E. The only reason these characters work for readers or viewers is because they are driven by human emotions. If a Cabbage-Patch doll lies on a floor all day, I'm not moved emotionally. However, make it have fears and dreams and ambitions the way Buzz Lightyear and Woody do, and I'm hooked for hours. Watching a garbage truck fill and empty all day is not my idea of entertainment, but give me a vehicle with a face, an attitude, and a challenge, as with Lightning McQueen, and I'm on board all the way.

The Wicked Witch of the West may be a make-believe character, but her lust for Dorothy's shoes and her evil desire for power are human characteristics everyone can comprehend. The Little Engine That Could may be steel, coal, and steam, but his driving ambition to conquer his weakness and cross the mountain are worthy traits admired by all humans. No matter how unreal our central characters may be in regard to the actual world, they will still be accepted by readers if they have human traits readers can nod to and identify with—good or bad.

Third, ***the story needs to have a message.*** Yes, it is true that readers read fiction for entertainment. But an important part of being entertained is gaining a sense of having learned something or grown in a new way.

Reading Robert A. Heinlein's *Stranger in a Strange Land* presents us with an alien named Michael Valentine Smith, who travels to distant planets. Michael's honesty, simplicity, and decency transcend the fact that such a story could never actually happen. We are left with a lesson about the impact moral discipline can have on ourselves and on others.

Similarly, *The Island of Dr. Moreau* by H. G. Wells presents us with animals that have been given transplants of human blood and organs, causing them to walk upright and talk. Such a thing could never actually happen, but as we listen to the animals relate their woes about their imprisonment in cages, their beatings, and their treatment as misfits, we cannot help but ask ourselves if this is not similar to the treatment that oppressed people continue to receive in many societies and countries. These stories may be fantastic, but their messages are all too real.

## The Reality of Disbelief

We see then that fiction is logically ironic. Readers don't mind suspending disbelief as long as stories are contextually consistent, characters are motivated by human emotions, and messages are thought-provoking and identifiable. It sounds like double talk, but, alas, whoever said the human mind is balanced? It isn't, folks. And, thank goodness for that, or else we fiction writers would be unemployed.

"Hey, kids, what time is it?" Let's hope it remains "Howdy Doody time!" for a long, long while.

# Nitty-Gritty Tip 4
## Once *Before* a Time—
## Creating Prequels

**Sequels to stories** have been around for centuries, but trying to imagine what had happened *before* the story of record started is a rather new concept. In fact, the term *prequel* was added to the dictionary only in the past couple of decades. George Lucas began his *Star Wars* series with Episode IV, thus implying that at least three prequels would be necessary to fill in the backstory of the first movie. He went on to make episodes V and VI, and then went back to make I, II and II.

Indeed, movies seem to have been the first to capitalize on prequels. The *Indiana Jones* franchise released a phenomenally successful prequel after the first movie in the series had been made.

Sometimes, both movies *and* novels capitalize on prequels. The novel *Jane Eyre* has been made into a movie half a dozen times, but when its prequel novel was written, *Wide Sargasso Sea*, that book quickly became a movie, too.

The Jenkins-LaHaye *Left Behind* series spun off a prequel series: *Before They Were Left Behind*. The stage musical *Wicked* is a prequel to the novel (and movie), *The Wizard of Oz*.

Prequels are the rage these days. But how do you write one?

## Who Owns the Property?

If you decide to write a prequel, you first need to make sure that the original work is now in public domain or is something you personally wrote. For example, you could write the prequel to *A Christmas Carol* by Charles Dickens but not to *The Firm* by John Grisham. You have a variety of options in brainstorming a prequel.

1. **Consider a fleshing out of implied information.** Using our previous example, what information could you draw upon to enhance and expand on what we already know of Ebenezer Scrooge's early life, as alluded to during the visit by the Ghost of Christmas Past? Additionally, what could you make up about the courtship and marriage of Bob Cratchit and his wife, the birth of their children, and the earliest years of Tiny Tim, already knowing that the Cratchits are poor and Tim is disabled? Basically, you would be embellishing on provided information to formulate a backstory for each character.

2. **Look at the story from a new point of view.** How would the prequel of *A Christmas Carol* be told if it were from the viewpoint of Scrooge's young fiancée, whom he deserted in order to pursue money? How would it be told from the viewpoint of Scrooge's sister, who died not long after giving birth to a son, Scrooge's nephew and only remaining blood

relative? Or, perhaps most intriguing of all, how would it be told from the viewpoint of Marley, Scrooge's now-deceased business partner? The angles, nuances, viewpoints, opinions, judgments, and perspectives could be endless. And who says you couldn't have a prequel told from multiple points of view?

3. **Examine your throw-away notes.** If you've written a novel, you know that you've had to cut scenes, delete passages of dialogue, and pare several chapters. It hurts to do that. In fact, in writing my novels, I couldn't part with that material. By looking back at your deletes and discards, you might find foundational storylines for a prequel.

4. **Interview the supporting characters.** If you wish to tell a prequel from the omniscient point of view, that doesn't mean you cannot draw material from myriad sources. Before writing the prequel to *A Christmas Carol*, you could make a list of all the secondary characters. Then, you could conduct imaginary interviews with them. There would be no wrong answers, for nobody really knows *how* Bob Cratchit was hired by Scrooge or *when* he first started working for him or *what* the range of his duties was or exactly *how much* his meager salary was or *why* Bob didn't seek employment elsewhere. By conducting five to ten in-depth interviews, you would have a wealth of material to use as the foundation of your prequel.

## Overcoming Intimidation.

Obviously, it seems a bit audacious to assume that one would be on a level with Charles Dickens or Leo Tolstoy or Jack London or George Orwell or Mark Twain and could write a prequel to the works of these authors.

Well, then, be audacious. When *Scarlett* was published as the sequel to *Gone with the Wind*, half the critics loved it and were excited to see the continuation of the story, but the other half loathed it and said it was a pathetic, poor imitation of the Margaret Mitchell masterpiece. Any prequel or sequel you write of a classic will suffer the same fate. Don't let that hamper your ambitions.

106

An actor who decides to play Hamlet cannot allow himself to be daunted by critics saying, "But that was already done to perfection by Laurence Olivier and Kenneth Branagh and Richard Burton and Mel Gibson and Michael Redgrave." The actor has to say, "And here, then, is my rendition of it."

Prequel writers must have the same chutzpah.

## Nitty-Gritty Tip 5
### Keep Readers Hooked Through Subplots

**If you were** to tell your life story in a basic, linear manner, it would be predictable and boring. You'd say something such as, "I was born in Detroit, where I went to school until I was ten, then my folks moved to Bay City, where I lived until I finished college, then I went into the army for two years, came out, got married, went to graduate school, had two kids, got a job teaching, and today I'm a grandfather."

In real life we get sideswiped by numerous unexpected events. The above vignette is actually my life story in one sentence. However, what would make it far more interesting would be the subplots in my life—I got a job as a young reporter and landed an interview with Johnny Cash...I was wounded in the face during the Vietnam War... my daughter was born with a complete heart block and remained for twelve days in intensive care...my son became a Marine and spent eight months in Iraq and Kuwait during Operation Desert Shield ...I got my doctorate and wrote more than sixty books.

That is the function of subplots in a novel. They offer unexpected twists. They provide moral lessons about perseverance or faith or endurance. They pivot the action from a steady flow of events to a radically unexpected—but totally believable—new event. In short, they add more intrigue to a story, and readers accept them because that is the way life actually does unfold.

## Populating the Subplot

In my co-written novel *The Gift,* protagonist Ian Moore has the ability to transfuse time from one person to another. His quest is to find a worthy successor to whom to pass along the gift before he dies. However, subplots show Ian being pursued by people who wish to use his powers for their own benefit. An aging multimillionaire wants to force Ian to make him young again. A physician wants to find Ian and learn the medical applications of what Ian can do. An aggressive investigative journalist wants be the one to reveal Ian's powers to the world and make himself famous.

As we see Ian from the perspectives of these secondary characters, we learn about his backstory, his motivations, and his beliefs. It would be hard to gain all this information from the central character himself, but deriving it from people involved in subplots makes it accessible and believable. Additionally, the emotional ties between Ian and the secondary characters give greater depth to the plot.

I don't believe in coming up with a main plot and then inventing random subplots to inject into the story. Instead, I try to think of how subplots can be woven into the main story as ways of providing comic relief or character empathy or threats of evil or moments of victory that are all part and parcel of the overarching story. If placed correctly, they can slow the narrative drive in a natural way, making the reader wait for the main story's resolution while staying interested in the progress or outcome of one or more subplots. One good test of the appropriateness of a subplot's inclusion in your synopsis and outline is to ask the question, "If I pulled this entire subplot out of the novel, would it leave a noticeable gap?" If your answer is, "Well, not really," then toss out that entire subplot.

A good subplot can reduce the responsibility of the main plot to keep the reader vested in all the details. If readers stay with one or two key characters page after page, the story becomes either tedious or morose. Old Westerns would insert a break ("Meanwhile back at the ranch…") so that the audience could change venues, focus on different characters, and be given a break from the intensity of an impending ambush. However, even a break from the main action can serve to intensify the pressure on the main character. True, Roy Rogers may escape the Indian attack, but unbeknownst to him, rustlers steal his cattle while he's away from the ranch. Thus, as the story advances, things get worse, not better, for the key character, and many of his or her challenges will come from events developing in the subplots.

## Drafting the Subplots

After you have developed profiles of your main protagonist and antagonist—and possibly a love interest too—you can focus on the secondary characters: sidekicks, bosses, apprentices, students, coworkers, neighbors, clients. Why are they in the story, and how will their challenges relate to the more dominating challenges being faced by the main character?

Sheriff Andy Taylor was the central character in Mayberry, but if Opie was being bullied at school or Aunt Bee was worried about competing in the county fair pie contest or Barney Fife was having dating problems with Thelma Lou, they all turned to Andy to make things tranquil once again. Andy was a peacemaker, both literally and figuratively. The lesser characters didn't dominate in the plots as much as he did, but their interactions with him were natural, continuous, and entertaining.

It has been said that people shape events, and events shape people. As you give thought to how your main and secondary characters came to be who and what they are, subplots will begin to take shape in your mind. Jot down notes. Pose questions. Speculate about scenarios. Play what-if games. Consider where your characters live, what era they live in, what their key concerns are. Events will then surface, and the way your characters decide to respond to them will form your subplots. After all…subplot-events in your life made you turn out the way you are now, right? So, apply the same logic, and you will be able to develop logical and interesting subplots for your novel.

# Nitty-Gritty Tip 6
## How to Write Series Novels—Linking Past to Present

**The mystery-romance** novels I co-authored under the pen name of Leslie Holden were published in a series and contained recurring characters. I found it to be a real challenge to give new readers the background of what has happened in previous novels while not boring faithful readers who have already read those books.

We couldn't simply say, "In our last thrill-packed episode, Joan threatened suicide when Jack…" So, instead, what had to be done was make the background information part of the new plot so that it appeared to be a springboard for pending action rather than a retelling of old news.

Here are the six techniques I use most often to fill readers in on the background:

1. **Interrogations**. When a police officer interrogates a suspect, readers will expect him to tell the suspect what the police already know about the crime or investigation. After all, the cop has to justify why he had the suspect brought down to the police station.

The reader then gets to listen in as the cop says, "On October 18 you were seen in…" and "Your landlady told us you moved out on…" and "Four people at your job heard you threaten your boss after you were told…." As this scene builds toward the next expected point of action in the novel—the suspect's arrest and imprisonment—readers are given a complete summary of the character's previous actions.

2.  **Trial Scenes.** In the novel *The Caribbean Conspiracy* (Harvest House, 1987; Whitaker House, 2015), it was my job to distill information from two previous novels into the climax of this third novel. By using a courtroom trial to do this, I was able to parade select witnesses before the jury—and the readers. These witnesses explained what they had seen, heard, were told, and remembered about previous incidents. This kept the action going while also filling in the background.

3.  **Newspapers and Scrapbooks.** In the TV version of Alex Haley's *Roots*, Haley (played by James Earl Jones) goes into a library and reads old newspapers on microfilm in order to discover the history of his parents, grandparents, and other relatives. The viewer gets to read the material with Haley and, thus, get caught up on any episodes he or she may have missed.

    Characters in a novel can discover old newspapers or family scrapbooks in an attic or garage or basement. As they read the clippings aloud, the reader will also hear the news about the winning touchdown eight years before or the wedding in the campus chapel the previous spring.

4.  **Computer Records.** In *The Pelican Brief*, John Grisham's characters obtain computer printouts of students' college class schedules in order to find out what they are studying, where they live, and who they've worked for. In the novel *The Compton Connection* (Harvest House, republished as *Nashville Nights* by Whitaker House, 2015), I had a CIA director call up a computer record of a missing US soldier in Vietnam. As the

director reads selected parts of the record, the readers are given a thumbnail sketch of what happened to this soldier in the previous novel, *The Legacy of Lillian Parker* (Harvest House, 1986; Whitaker House, 2015).

5. **Media Interviews.** Having a main character in a book appear on a radio or TV talk show or consent to be interviewed for a newspaper or magazine will provide repartee that quickly summarizes the character's previous achievements, as well as announce his or her new plans.

6. **Partial Conversations.** Snatches of dialogue can be sprinkled into chapters to provide clues to and insights on previous events. Lines such as, "I was so sorry to hear you lost the town council election last November" or "Your cousin told me you retired last year and turned the store over to your daughter" or "How has your mother been doing since your dad passed away last summer?" tell a story in themselves. I once wrote a chapter in which a waiter heard a dozen of these one-liners as he walked through a party. In that one scene my readers learned what had occurred to these characters in my previous novel.

Let me add a word of caution. Previous-event summarizations that work well in a visual medium may not work equally as well in print. For example, the opening scene of the movie *MacArthur* has Gregory Peck delivering a long speech to the cadets of West Point as a way of providing background about MacArthur's life. That same technique is used in the movie *The Closer*, which opens with a long speech by Danny Aiello. Because the camera angles keep changing and the point of view continually moves from the speaker to the audience and back again, this proves to be an effective way to begin a movie. However, to open a novel with the transcript of a ten-page speech would be deadly.

Similarly, an overlap summary/transition that works well in movies doesn't work at all in novels. For instance, in the beginning of the movie *Back to the Future II* we are presented with nothing more than a replaying of the final eight minutes of the original *Future* movie. But the action is fast-moving and informative and it immediately establishes the premise of the sequel. I can't imagine, however, that a publisher would take kindly to the idea of beginning a new novel with a reprinting of the last chapter of the book in the series that preceded it.

Developing a series is a wonderful way of compounding your income. If someone reads the third book in your series and loves it, he or she will want to buy books one and two. Your task, therefore, is to provide enough information about the previous two books that a reader jumping into the series at book three won't be lost, yet you won't want to give away so much of the previous information that it will be unnecessary for readers to read those previous books.

It's a balancing act to please the reader with a minimum of necessary facts while also teasing the reader into wanting to go back and get the full story. That's the secret—please and tease, please and tease, please and tease.

# Chapter 6
# Spot-on Characters, Dialogue, and Settings

## Spot On Tip 1
### Ask All the
### Wrong Questions

**When I went** in to defend my doctoral dissertation in English, five committee members were ready to fire questions at me. They included a doctor of linguistics, a doctor of British literature, a doctor of American literature, a doctor of English studies—and a doctor of musicology. The latter member was no oversight or misplacement. You see, PhD committees at most universities have what is known as an "odd person out."

The logic behind this is that people in your own area of study are going to ask you questions familiar to everyone in that field. But that doesn't necessarily mean someone outside of your field will be able to read your dissertation and understand it. And if that's the case, the dissertation's contribution to the overall field of knowledge will be vastly limited. So, having a layperson ask for clearer interpretations of key points, needed background on certain issues, and definitions of specific terms will allow the writer to see where he or she has been ambiguous, short-sighted, or pompous.

I'm convinced this "odd person out" is a useful alter ego to have when you begin to sketch out your fictional characters for stories or plays. The usual practice—and I'm not against this—is to establish the backstory and key features of central characters. To that end, you usually write out a character's physical description and personality traits, as well as important facts about the person's educational and occupational training and livelihood, military history, family tree, and avocations and hobbies. If it seems pertinent, I sometimes also add information about the person's religious beliefs, political leanings, social-club memberships, and dreams and ambitions.

## Other Points of View

Once you have created profiles for your central fiction characters, you will immediately see that readers are going to expect a certain pattern of behavior that reflects each character's make-up. For example, if a character has earned a master's degree and passed the state teacher's exam, readers will assume she won't be saying "ain't" and "don't got none" or use street slang. Conversely, a poorly educated immigrant will be expected to speak broken English, have a limited knowledge of American history, and be working at a low-paying job. Behavior outside these parameters would be illogical, irrational, and unbelievable.

But therein lies the rub. How do you create *realistic* characters who can still surprise your readers and propel a plot forward? That's where your "odd person out" begins to ask all the wrong questions. Here are sample questions that could be asked of any fictional character, but usually aren't:

- Why did this character decide to walk to work today rather than drive?

- Why is this character terrified of car washes?

- What tragic mistake can't this character forgive himself or herself for?

- Why has this person cut off all communication with other family members?

115

- How would this person respond to winning a million-dollar lottery?

- Why does this person visit the church's small cemetery each Thursday?

The purpose of this exercise is to probe into areas that most people try to hide, disguise, or ignore. By asking atypical questions, you are forced to examine your character from different points of view. The character can still walk and talk and dress like a poorly educated immigrant, but now he will stand out from the crowd because he will have a sense of mission that makes him interesting to readers.

If you consider Hester Prynne in *The Scarlet Letter*, the profile might read as follows: "Colonial American, New Englander, female, Puritan, Caucasian, early-20s, unmarried, seamstress." That's a standard profile of half the women of that era. However, to create a plot, you must ask an atypical question, such as, "Who got her pregnant?" or "What great secret is she withholding, even to the point of causing her to be ostracized by the rest of the colony?" or "Why is her mode of dress different from everyone else's?" Answer any one of these questions, and you'll have a character who is still in line with the reader's expectations, yet has surprises that will propel the plot forward.

It seems as though the contrasting elements of needing to create a "stock" character who is "uniquely challenged" are incompatible. However, readers like stock characters with whom they can identify, but the unique circumstances that push these stock characters into unexpected trials, challenges, and adventures are what will sustain the readers' interest. You will discover these circumstances by asking off-the-wall, unexpected, atypical, "wrong" questions about your fictional characters.

**If your short** story or novel is finished but somehow doesn't seem to have sparks of uniqueness, you can improve it greatly during the second draft by making small but significant changes to the central character.

For example, in a story by one of my college students, the plot was captivating and the ending had a clever surprise, but something was missing. The central character was routine. I suggested the student revise the story and make the main character deaf. At first the student was baffled by such a suggestion, but when she followed my advice, the main character elicited new empathy. His struggles were more difficult, his success was less assured, and his behavior patterns were anything but normal. Now the story was far more interesting.

I gained this idea by reading short stories and watching movies in which characters are more distinctive because of a physical infirmity. Let's use one simple example, that of limping. In the space of fifteen minutes I came up with a list of thirty-four fictional characters known for having a pronounced limp.

Both Captain Ahab of *Moby Dick* and Long John Silver of *Treasure Island* are missing a lower leg due to an unfortunate encounter with a sea creature. On television programs that began in the 1950s we had Grandpa Amos McCoy (Walter Brennan) in *The Real McCoys* and Chester (Dennis Weaver) in *Gunsmoke* who had pronounced limps. Dr. Philip Carey, the main character in W. Somerset Maugham's classic novel *Of Human Bondage*, limps because of a birth defect that caused a club foot. Another physician, Dr. Kerry Weaver (Laura Innes), for twelve seasons of the TV show *ER,* used a cane and listed to one side when walking. In the opening episode of the PBS series *Sherlock*, Dr. John Watson had a psychosomatic limp that Holmes "cured" by getting the doctor so caught up in a case that he forgot to keep walking that way.

Kenny Rogers limped through all of *The Gambler* Western movies on TV. In the most recent movie remake of Elmore Leonard's short story "3:10 to Yuma," Paul Scallan (Christopher Bale) is missing a lower leg due to a wound from the Civil War and, thus, he hobbles through the entire movie. John Bates (Brendan Coyle), valet to Lord Grantham on the PBS series *Downton Abbey*, used a cane due to a leg injury he received in the Boer War.

Even in the TV series *Person of Interest*, there was a fascinating point of curiosity. In present-day scenes during the first few seasons, central character Harold Finch walked with a very pronounced limp. But in flashback scenes of Harold as a boy or as a youthful computer-science genius, he did not walk that way. Viewers had to guess how and when he was injured enough to leave him (a multibillionaire, no less) permanently disabled with rigid posture, unable to turn his head fully or walk with a steady gait.

## Making the Challenge More Intense

The reason physically challenged characters intrigue readers so much is because they present a quandary. We wonder, have they become fascinating individuals because their handicap forced them to overcome serious obstacles just to survive, or will the physical hindrance somehow eventually lead to their demise if they encounter situations in which all human faculties are required? We watch these people, study them, and try to learn from them. They constantly are in an adapt-or-die kind of environment, which heightens plot intensity.

It is important not to portray these individuals as pathetic, unless there is some sort of subsequent redeeming change in the person. For example, Lieutenant Dan in *Forrest Gump* truly is a pathetic individual—drunken, slovenly, abrasive, self-pitying, and spiteful. As a wheelchair-bound double-amputee Vietnam vet, his bitterness makes him hateful to everyone around him until Gump's love, loyalty, and friendship give Dan a new reason to live and be happy. He may still be bound to the wheelchair, but Dan no longer is emotionally handicapped. Good story.

So, the lesson is, don't portray challenged individuals until you understand how they are challenged. When I slipped on concrete, cracked my pelvic socket, and was in a wheelchair for three months, I learned firsthand what it was like to have someone else drive for me, open restroom doors for me, even tie my shoes. I came closer to understanding abandonment when people went to get coffee and left me sitting in the classroom alone. I understood personal frustration when, working in my office, I couldn't simply jump up to answer the phone, turn on a light, or sharpen my pencil. Since that time I've always offered help to anyone in a wheelchair. My sensitivity is borne of experience.

Thus, conduct interviews, do online research, and interview therapists. If you fully understand the challenges presented by specific injuries or diseases, you'll portray them honestly while introducing us to a character who is a survivor.

In giving a physical challenge to a fictional character, there is no element of mockery. Quite the opposite. Being able to solve crimes is impressive, but if you are wheelchair-bound, such as Chief Ironside (Raymond Burr) in *Ironside*, or you are a quadriplegic, such as Lincoln Rhyme (Denzel Washington) in *The Bone Collector*, it is even more impressive. Our admiration for such characters rises as they amaze us in more ways than one. (Note that in the original movie of *Rear Window*, the central character [Jimmy Stewart] was bound to a wheelchair, but in the remake, the plot intensity was greatly enhanced by making the central character [Christopher Reeve] a quadriplegic.)

The secret to getting readers to keep turning pages is to add plot intensity. If a physical challenge can be added to the regular problems of day-to-day life, plot intensity is automatically achieved.

Additionally, character empathy is assured. For a fiction writer, it's the best of both worlds.

⋯⋯⋯⬦⋯⋯⋯

## Spot On Tip 3
## When to Make Fictional Characters Versions of You—and When Not To

**When W. Somerset Maugham** wrote *Of Human Bondage* and Jack London wrote *Martin Eden*, by design their main male characters were based on their own lives. Like Maugham, fictional Philip Carey is a medical doctor, an avid reader, and a person who has a physical malady. (Carey has a club foot; Maugham had a terrible stutter he was never able to correct.) Similarly, like London, Martin Eden is a sailor, a self-taught author, and a person obsessed with becoming famous and wealthy.

In each of these books, the central character is also unlike its creator. Philip Carey spends years studying painting in Paris, and he loses all his investments in mine stocks, neither of which was true of Maugham. Martin Eden never marries (London married twice) and eventually commits suicide (not true of London, though his alcoholism did lead to a premature death).

Usually when a writer less skilled than Maugham or London tries to write the *roman à clef,* or autobiographical novel, it comes off as mundane or self-aggrandizing. Both are boring. However, many beginning writers tell me, "But I know myself best, so why not start there?" And the answer is, "Because, unlike Jack London, you probably have not hunted seals on the high seas, ventured into Alaska in search of gold, built your own ranch in Southern California, written twenty-seven successful novels and 190 published short stories, been a war correspondent in Mexico, Korea, Japan, and Russia, and built your own yacht and sailed it halfway around the world. In short, you don't have enough exciting personal material to draw from."

## No Alter Egos, Please

How do you create fictional characters who are definitely not a mirror image of yourself? To begin with, purposely give birth to a character who is your opposite. Change the skin color, hairstyle, sex, ethnicity, age, educational background, social environment, hobbies, world travels, life goals, and family ties. Put all the characteristics down on paper, examine them, and then see how such a character can be involved in a plot of mystery, romance, or adventure.

Next, do a bit of psychological introspection, asking yourself how you handle jealousy, envy, fear, anger, surprise, and shock. How can you make your fictional character respond differently? *Why* would he or she respond differently due to personal experiences, training, and/or outlook on life?

Next, consider activities and backstory. If you were in the Air Force, have your character be in the Marines. If you were in marching band in school, let your character be in the chess club. If you are now working as an insurance agent, let your character be a librarian or police officer or computer geek.

Finally, give your character some life experiences different from yours. Perhaps your character will have gone through a divorce or will have lost an eye in a car accident or will have won five million dollars in a lottery or will have kicked a game-winning field goal that is still talked about years later. Make the incident significant.

## Enlarge the Dynamics

One thing that helped give more breadth and depth to the characters in four of my novels was working with coauthor Holly G.

Miller. I created many of the characters for these novels, but Holly altered their personalities, appearances, attitudes, and behavior patterns to fit the needs of our plots. Thus, even if certain characters may have started off looking like clones of me, they didn't stay that way for long. Similarly, I have now co-authored a new novel with a different female writer, Diana Savage, and she too morphed the characters I created so they can better accommodate our goals for the plot. Thus, consider working with a coauthor if your characters continually come out as reflections of yourself.

Investigative research can also help you make your characters unique. If you decide to make a character be someone radically different from you, find a real-life person like that and shadow him or her for a few days. Take notes about body language, key vocabulary words and phrases, manner of dress, highs and lows of the job, stressors, work hours, colleague relationships, and work environments. Filter this factual material into the life and career of your character. The result will be someone unique, not just a watered-down version of you.

Additionally, allow your character to go where you fear to go, do what you are afraid to do, and explore what you dread to examine. It's safe to push yourself out of your comfort zone if you allow your avatar or renegade twin to do the dangerous stuff while you sit back and observe.

Fiction, by necessity, must be larger than life. The extraordinary is what fascinates us. As such, your daily regimen won't qualify as much of a plot. Instead, create someone unlike you through whom you can have challenges, ordeals, and quests that exceed your scope.

Who knows? The person you create may be able to experience the life you've always dreamed of. Okay…sell it.

**Writers who cannot** write good dialogue are like tone-deaf musicians. To help my writing students improve their tonal quality when writing dialogue, I have created several exercises. Here are a few of those exercises you can try with your writers club or critique group:

1. **Create an improvisational theatre.** Come up with a scene concept and then assign two or three people to talk through it, saying what comes naturally to them. Make an audio or video recording, and play it back later to identify the passages that ring true.

2. **Trade manuscripts and insert gems.** Take another writer's passage of dialogue and revise the lines by inserting a clever turn of phrase, some witty slang, a touch of dialect, a funny pun, a play on words, or a double entendre.

3. **Do an oral reading of someone's passage of dialogue while pretending to be a well-known actor.** If two men are arguing, ask one person to pretend to be Clint Eastwood and the other to be Bruce Willis or Tom Hanks or Nicholas Cage. If the participants are women, perhaps they could pretend to be Gwyneth Paltrow facing off with Scarlett Johansson or Sally Field or Maggie Smith. Often the way readers use nuances,

pauses, inflections, or even purposeful silences will reveal how dialogue can be revised to be more dramatic or better paced.

4. **Impersonate the style of dialogue made famous by a specific performer.** Similar to exercise 3, this exercise is a variation of the actor's interpretation. (Think Jack Webb as Sgt. Joe Friday in *Dragnet*: "Yes, ma'am...no, ma'am...just the facts, ma'am.")

5. **Collect snippets of great dialogue.** Certain TV shows, such as *The West Wing*, *M*A*S*H*, and *Downton Abbey*, are renowned for their caustic, surprising, dazzling, biting repartee. View episodes and make a collection of several of the great comebacks, shocking one-liners, and snappy barbs. Sitting with other writers, decide why these exchanges worked and how you can use those set-ups.

6. **Create a list of words that emphasize compression.** These words might include such adjectives as *refined, pruned, disciplined, truncated, shortened, specific, heightened*, and *condensed*. For example, you might want to use *heightened* drama by inserting screams, gasps, or some stuttering. You might want to *prune* dialogue by deleting all references to someone else's name by making it more obvious as to who is being addressed and who is responding.

7. **Repeat a format or venue or delivery mode.** Try to compose a passage of dialogue in which both characters are using the same syntactical device. For example, you could have two characters use only questions:

> "Why didn't you attend the class reunion?"

> "Did you miss me, darling?"

> "Well, you were cochairman, weren't you?"

> "And you think that means I have to collect everyone's ticket at the door?"

"Don't you ever think of anyone's needs but your own?"

"Why should I? Do you?"

Variations of this could make use of accusations, exclamations, compliments, demands, lies, monosyllables, retorts, taunts, or witticisms.

8. **Create misdirected statements**. Sometimes having two characters talk, but having them on totally different comprehension levels, can be entertaining:

    "You're still wet behind the ears, sonny."

    "Of course I am. I've just won an Olympic gold medal in swimming."

9. **Insert stage business**. Examine a passage of dialogue to see how a nonverbal signal, such as a hand gesture, a double-take, a raised eyebrow, or a head scratching, might provide a "beat" between spoken lines and provide an emotional implication at the same time. Often, actions do speak louder than words.

10. **Eliminate adverbs**. Go through passages of dialogue and replace adverbs found in attributions with either better dialogue or actions that show the emotions. Instead of writing that Mary spoke *emphatically*, have Mary say, "And I'm going to keep coming here each day until I get my money back!" It's much more dramatic to hear her emphatic wording than to be told secondhand that she was speaking forcefully.

Dialogue doesn't have to be static, predictable, or bland. By exploring diverse methods of creating sparkling dialogue, you can make your spoken exchanges something readers will talk about when recommending your book to others.

**When one of** my recent books was about to be released, I received a call from my publisher. "You're saving us a lot of money," he said.

My response was instinctive. "Add it to my next royalty check."

"I'm serious, man. We hired a scriptwriter to convert your novel to a script for an audio book. She had it back to us in three days. She said your dialogue was so natural, she pretty much just transcribed it."

"You know what they say: 'If it ain't on the page, it ain't on the stage.'"

"Well," he said, "yours *is* on the page, so we're puttin' it on the stage."

### Act One, Scene One

Although novels, short stories, and works of narrative nonfiction are venues of the mind, I try to write dialogue as though my readers will be in an audience listening to a performance. It forces me to keep the dialogue crisp, witty, poignant, and supported by the right stage business. Let me share with you some tips from scriptwriting that will enhance your prose.

Begin by reading and studying other writers' scripts. And by that I mean reading them aloud. When I was in graduate school, one of my profs made us read out loud in class. We read long passages from plays by George Bernard Shaw, Lillian Hellman, Arthur Miller, Tennessee Williams, Thornton Wilder, Samuel Beckett, and Agatha Christie. I was amazed at how this approach to understanding literature also served to sharpen my ear in regard to writing dialogue for my short stories. I still do this today with TV and movie scripts, musicals, and stage dramas. You can do likewise by obtaining play collections from the library or downloading public domain scripts from the Internet.

## Try a Flip-Flop

If you're not confident about how to make a scene dramatic enough, you can surprise readers by doing a flip-flop. In scriptwriting this is called role reversal. A normal scene would have a mother going berserk because her seventeen-year-old daughter has come in two hours after curfew. But think about how much more intense the scene would be if the teenager were admonishing the mother for coming in late:

"You couldn't call or text to let me know you were okay?"

"It's a school night. I thought you'd be in bed."

"You've been a single mom for nine years, and you think I'm not going to want to hear about your first date?"

"It was just dinner with a friend, sweetheart."

"You've been gone seven hours, Mom. That was more than just dinner. Why are you so late?"

You can write a whole scene in the standard way, but then you can swap your characters' roles. What if the employee argued with her boss against giving raises to the employees...or the teacher argued with her principal, insisting teachers needed to spend more time after school fixing bulletin boards and preparing lesson plans... or the insurance agent tried to convince the customer he didn't need to purchase a $250,000 policy? To readers, role reversal is so unexpected, it compels them to see how the scene will unfold. It's edgy, surprising, and captivating.

## Have Dialogue Define Characters

If an episode in your novel is lying flat, or if the narrative drive of your plot starts to fizzle, enliven things by having a character explode onto the scene. When Cruella de Vil arrives at the young couple's apartment intent on confiscating all 101 Dalmatians, she bursts into the room in a whirlwind of total domination. Her hair is flying, her arms are flailing, her cigarette ashes are flinging. She wails and screeches as she bounces around the room counting the puppies.

Cruella doesn't merely talk, she bellows commands, insisting the dogs be rounded up, turned over to her, and taken to her limousine. Her volume is high, her words are caustic, and her behavior is flamboyant. There is an immediate new intensity to the overall plot. *What* Cruella says and *how* she says it instantly define her as the villain, someone to fear and hate and distrust. (Note: Don't you just love how her name contains the words *cruel* and *devil*?")

You can do something similar. A drill sergeant can burst into a barracks at 5:00 a.m. booming orders. An ambulance team can ram through the doors of an emergency room calling out vital signs for a patient being wheeled inside. A judge can suddenly lose her temper, slam her gavel, and lecture the defense attorney. In each instance, the power and volume of the dialogue will define the role of the person speaking, as well as intensify the energy of the scene.

## Think Uniqueness, Not Accents

When I'm sitting in an airport during layovers, I listen to the way people around me talk, and I take notes. I don't try to capture a German accent or a Southern drawl as much as I try to record the uniqueness of the speech patterns. How do people pronounce specific words? What words do they like to use, and which words do they repeat frequently? I find myself jotting down idioms, contractions, word order (syntax), and even ways grammar rules are broken. I sometimes transcribe overheard conversations and later read them aloud as though I'm an actor trying to learn lines in a play. It puts people inside my head who don't sound like me. This leads to diversity in my fictional characters' voices.

## Talking the Talk

When dialogue works well, it gives vitality to scenes and definition to characters. Often, it has to be rewritten many times before it sounds natural. However, revision is worth the effort because readers return to authors who can talk the talk of insightful, entertaining dialogue.

## Spot On Tip 6
## How to Nail Your
## Fiction Settings

**I've worked for** many years writing and selling freelance travel articles to newspapers and magazines, and more recently, to e-zines. It's a double opportunity. I can explore a new locale doing research for a short story or novel and wind up getting to deduct my expenses and also earn bylines and cash by writing about the place. So, thinking now as fiction writers, let's look at how to investigate a new setting.

A trick I learned from my studies of Jack London was first to summarize the entire locale in a single sentence. When London wrote, "The Yukon, where to lose a glove was to lose a hand," he not only was summarizing the weather, but he also initiated the plot conflict.

Likewise, when C. S. Lewis wrote that Narnia was "always winter, but never Christmas," he was establishing the weather as well as the mood and the heavy intensity of the setting.

## Record the Setting

Before you leave your locale after a day of exploring, questioning, and researching, sit for a moment, concentrate on what you feel was the most emotional aspect of the day, and then attempt to encapsulate it in one sentence. This will be the bull's-eye of your story's setting.

Next, make a list of the unique sensual impressions this place made on you:

- Did you hear distinctive sounds, such as bells from an ancient church or low-flying seagulls or screaming market vendors or mopeds darting in and out of narrow streets?

- Were there arresting scents, aromas, or stenches, such as tractor diesel fumes or salt-laden ocean breezes or smoky fire pits or pine forests?

- Did you experience unique tactile sensations, such as handmade Amish quilts or burning-hot sandy beaches or scratchy Irish sweaters or damp morning fog?

- Did you encounter marvelous tastes, such as rich French pastries or strong Brazilian coffee or crispy Canadian bacon or tangy California oranges?

- Were you impressed by one-of-a-kind visual images, such as the balancing rocks at Garden of the Gods or tons of flowing water at Niagara Falls or snowfalls in July at Denali Park or endless miles of sand in the Sahara?

Get it all down before it escapes you, and don't use lame expressions such as "breathless vistas" or "never-ending tides" or "majestic mountains" or "nature's masterpiece."

Next, take one of everything not nailed down, such as restaurant menus, labeled books of matches, postcards, brochures, city maps, flyers, advertisements, photos.... They will stimulate your memory when you mentally revisit the place one day to write your fiction setting.

When you begin to sketch out your scenes, remember that, although they will be fictional, they will also need to be realistic. Often what helps me when doing research is to jot down comments made by other people who are also visiting the same place. Seeing the identical things through other sets of eyes can provide fresh perspectives.

For example, when I was registering at the historic Cliff House Hotel in Manitou Springs, Colorado, a guest next to me was told his room was not ready. He replied, "You built it in 1889. How can it not be ready?" I thought that was hilarious, so I used that line in my travel article and later in a short story.

I also like to talk to housekeeping employees, restaurant bussers and servers, shuttle drivers, desk clerks, and tour guides. They've been at that location a lot longer than I have, so they can provide background, humorous anecdotes, and different points of view.

Once you are back home and ready to create that setting in a work of fiction, look again at all the souvenirs and paraphernalia you accrued. Also, review your notes about the sensual impressions you recorded. Then close your eyes, mentally go back to the period of time you were there, walk the streets, visualize the buildings and rooms, and listen again to the voices of the people you encountered.

Once you are in the zone, start creating your setting. It will become real to you, and, thus, you'll make it real to your readers.

## Ensuring Authenticity

Nothing is more aggravating than reading a book or watching a movie in which the so-called locale is presented wrong in every aspect. For example, the Spielberg movie *Close Encounters of the Third Kind* supposedly takes place in Muncie, Indiana. Well, that's ridiculous. In one scene Richard Dreyfus enters the city electrical plant, which is the size of something that would run Los Angeles. (Muncie has a squirrel on a rotating belt.)

In another scene Dreyfus looks out over a cliff into a deep valley. The only "valley" in Muncie is a small dip in a street where it passes under a viaduct. The police uniforms are all wrong, the newspaper banner is incorrect, even the milk cartons aren't portrayed accurately. Worst of all, there is a scene in which the characters stop to pay a toll at a booth leading into Ohio. For crying out loud, who would pay money to enter Ohio?

For anyone who has lived in Indiana, that movie's locale-fiasco makes it impossible to concentrate on the plot. You, as a writer, do not want to be a perpetrator of something like that. In fact, you want to be praised for your sense of verisimilitude. I have received letters from people who have read my short stories and novels in which I've used Vietnam as a setting, and they have praised me for getting the weather right, the jungle vegetation right, and the language right.

Well, why not? I spent a year there as a sergeant in the army during the war, and I made a lot of notes and took a lot of photos. I know whereof I write. And discerning readers recognize when a setting rings true.

Making sure you nail your fictional locales will mark you as a professional writer.

# Chapter 7
# Develop a Support Team

**Support Team Tip 1**
**My Biggest Mistake**
**as a**
**Beginning Writer**

**As a high** school senior at age eighteen, I knew I wanted to be a professional writer. The problem was, I didn't know anyone who was a professional writer. I didn't know any editors or literary agents or publishers, either. So, I committed a terrible mistake and tried to make it on my own. As I tell my college writing students today, "Freelance doesn't mean you work alone, and it doesn't mean you work for free."

Although I majored in English in college, my literature teachers knew nothing about copyright laws, manuscript marketing, book proposals, or movie options. As a result, I sent out manuscripts to a wide variety of publications with large and small circulations, and I spent years getting mostly rejections slips and not knowing why. Finally—more by fool luck than on purpose—I had a chance meeting with a literary agent who took pity on me and agreed to spend ten minutes reading some of my sample manuscripts.

The man was absolutely vicious. He pulled out a red pen and bloodied my pages as he admonished me, "No, no, no! *Never* type your titles in all capital letters. *Never* leave a right or left margin that isn't at least one inch wide. *Never* have two speakers use dialogue in the same paragraph." On and on he railed and slashed and criticized, all the while rolling his eyes and shaking his head at my incompetence.

That was simultaneously the saddest and the happiest day of my writing career. It was devastating because I could see that for years no one had looked at anything I'd written and considered it professional. However, it was joyful because at least now I knew what I was doing wrong, and I could start doing things right.

After that eye-opening experience, I immediately joined a writers club so I could be taught by people who were in the game. Additionally, I started attending writers conferences so I could network with editors and agents—the key people who could bring me into the big leagues of publishing. In time, I became a newspaper columnist, then a successful magazine freelance writer, then a contributing editor with five magazines, and finally the author of dozens of books.

The writing business is not all that different from other businesses. Here are the keys to success when you start out:

1. Establish a network of contacts—via referrals or internships or club memberships—who are already successful in the field you want to enter.

2. Find mentors who will offer advice, critique your work and give feedback, and guide you in setting your career goals.

3. Seek guidance from distant experts by reading books, listening to audio training recordings, and viewing educational videos.

Even the Lone Ranger had Tonto. Don't go it alone. Get connected.

## Support Team Tip 2
### Grow with
### a Mentor

**In writing circles** and other areas, we hear a lot about mentoring today. But it's not a new idea. The most dynamic leaders of the Old Testament sought one or more mentors to guide the development of their careers. Joshua had Moses. David had Nathan. Elisha had Elijah.

I too can attest to the value of mentors. When I was a high school senior, my English teacher, Neil Ringle, gave me lists of books to read, edited my manuscripts, and encouraged me to write for the school literary magazine.

In college, my adviser and teacher Lorine Parks pushed me into becoming a reporter for the college newspaper, helped me select the courses that would best prepare me for a career as a freelance writer, and worked elbow to elbow with me to improve my writing by line-editing my papers.

Today, I have close friends in the field of writing to whom I can turn for advice, encouragement, teaching, and perspective. To grow your writing career, consider finding mentors to help you too.

### Selecting Mentors

To choose mentors, begin by listing what is needed both in your personal life and in your professional career. For life skills, you may need help in time management, financial balance, or health issues. For career skills, you may need help mastering writing mechanics, marketing your finished manuscripts, or building a national platform.

Sometimes one mentor can help you in all of these areas, but more likely, you will need two or even three mentors. For example, I used to meet three times a week with a personal trainer who talked to me about maintaining a proper diet, who guided my physical workouts, and who advised me on getting proper rest. However, I have a different person to whom I turn when I need someone to proofread and copyedit my manuscripts, maintain my website, and help me with national speaking engagements.

Because the best advisers are successful people themselves, it will not be easy to secure their guidance. You may have to pay for it, as I did with my personal trainer. You may have to barter for it, as I do with fellow writers when we edit each other's writings. You may have to merit it, as I did when I was a young reporter and worked extra hours and took on extra assignments to prove to my editors that I was worthy of the time they were investing to teach me techniques of investigative journalism and deadline writing.

Approach the person you feel will be of greatest help to you (successful author, insightful teacher, influential literary agent) and with humility ask for an initial meeting. Be transparent in saying, "I want to develop the skills and abilities I see you have mastered. If you could work with me in whatever time you can spare, I promise I won't disappoint you."

In your first meeting, present a list of your goals that you feel will help you advance as a person and as a writer. Ask for direction. Are there people you should meet, books you should read, workshops you should attend, connections you should make? Walk away with some specific suggestions, then amaze the potential mentor by returning with proof that you have followed that advice, e.g., typed summaries of the key points found in the recommended books or quotes from the workshop you attended.

If you encounter resistance in trying to set up an initial meeting with a potential mentor, see if you can get a referral. You can write or phone the potential mentor and say, "Your friend Mike Davis suggested I contact you." Or "Having studied under the same professor you studied under at City University, I was hoping we could meet sometime."

Don't demand too much right away. When people call and ask to take me to coffee, I am put off if they hand me a five-hundred-page manuscript, hoping I'll edit it for free. I also am put off by people who either brag endlessly about their potential or who continually put themselves down and play the part of the victim who has never been given a fair chance.

I am eager to hear what you have accomplished thus far, where you are headed, and why you feel I might be of help to you. Also, like most mentors, I am open to bribes. As author and editor Lin Johnson tells students at the college where I direct the Professional Writing major, "It's always good to send a thank-you letter to editors—and chocolate."

Having a mentor can reveal shortcuts to you, open doors for you, protect your blind sides, keep you focused, hold you accountable, push you to new levels, and channel your energies and talents toward success.

One stick can easily be broken over the knee. Two sticks are sturdier, stronger, and more durable. Don't go it alone. You need a mentor.

## Support Team Tip 3
## Your Critique Partners

**We writers need** feedback. We need people who can read our manuscripts and point out things we haven't noticed, such as grammar and punctuation errors, sloppy transitions, illogical dialogue, missing backstory, and confused plotting. However, selecting people we can turn to and trust to give honest feedback and knowledgeable analysis must be done with discernment and professionalism.

Finding a critique partner involves searching. You can join a local writers club and discover who the meticulous proofreaders and experienced writers are. You can become part of an online forum and do some test runs with other writers who want to swap and critique manuscripts. You can take a continuing education class in writing at a local college and meet other developing writers. You can hire professional copyeditors. You can go to a writers conference and attend night-owl sessions where writers read their manuscripts aloud and seek feedback.

Once you find someone you think will be helpful to you, it's good to set ground rules at the start. Perhaps you prefer strict confidentiality and will not want this other person to show your work to anyone else. Perhaps you will have expectations that feedback will be given within a set time period. Perhaps you will need specific explanations about any changes made to your manuscripts. Perhaps you are the kind of thin-skinned writer who needs to hear the good news (praise) before you hear the bad news (criticism). Communicate these requirements up front. Get off to a good start with your partner, and, conversely, be sensitive to the requests and preferences of this partner as you evaluate his or her work.

Whether you meet in person, over Skype, or via e-mail or other electronic-communication medium, make the most of your time. After you receive an edited manuscript, go over the corrections and the suggested revisions carefully. Let it all stew for a couple of days. Then, make a list of specific questions. You may not have recognized a certain editing symbol or understood why a line of dialogue was rewritten or comprehended why an entire paragraph was struck. As your partner responds, take notes so you won't keep making the same mistakes in the future.

The longer you work as a writer, the more you will discover that various people have different specialties that can be of help to you in different situations. For example, my friend Lin Johnson is one of the sharpest writers and editors I know. Nevertheless, even she uses diverse critique partners. She has one person who proofreads the final draft copy of the magazine for which she is editor. She has two other people who partner with her in running the Write to Publish conference, and they proofread the brochures and conference materials.

I have similar practices. My wife Rose has a master's degree in education and is a licensed teacher. Before word processors, she also was my administrative assistant and typist for many years. As such, before I ever turn in a new book to my agent or publisher, I ask Rose to read the whole manuscript to check spelling, grammar, punctuation, syntax, transitions, and continuity.

However, Diana Savage, who serves as webmaster for my blog and website (dochensley.com) also reads the manuscript to make sure it is in correct *Chicago Manual* style, and she gives me an outside reader's opinion of the content.

Then, of course, my agent eventually offers feedback regarding marketability, narrative flow, and takeaway value. Each of these specialists, as noted earlier, protects my blind sides. If you are fortunate to discover the perfect critique partner, do all you can to nurture that relationship.

When I co-authored four novels and three nonfiction books with Holly G. Miller, she was the senior editor of *The Saturday Evening Post* and a staff columnist for more than twenty years for *Today's Christian Woman* and *Country Gentleman*. Holly was a ruthless editor, but in working with her, I learned how to be meticulous in my research and writing. Over the course of more than thirty years, we've team-taught writing workshops more than two hundred fifty times.

Holly will joke that it is a good thing she and I live one hundred miles apart because sometimes we are so bluntly honest in evaluating each other's work, it takes a day or two to heal from the wounds. But, the point is, we can trust each other to give precise, accurate, valuable evaluations. We don't pull punches. Yet, we also are quick to praise the other person for well-written passages.

Holly and I work together maybe three times a year now, but we stay in touch via technology during the interims. Professionally, we are equals, but we are not clones. She is female, from the East Coast originally, has a very rich background in journalism...and is left-handed. I am male, from the Midwest, have a degree in classic literature and linguistics...and am right-handed. We bring different skill sets and perspectives to the table when we critique each other or teach together. If you can find someone like that, you will be blessed.

Developing a turtle-shell hide is one of the qualities that makes a writer succeed. We all need to have our writing evaluated by competent second readers. Usually, they will make us look better than we really are. I'm certainly all in favor of that, so I'm going to get my wife to proofread this, and then I'll submit it to my editor.

## Support Team Tip 4
### Offering the
### Blemished Lamb—
### Why Editing Is Crucial

**Here is a** sad but true story. A few years ago, a would-be author approached me at a writers conference and asked me to take a look at the first chapter of her nonfiction book manuscript. She said she wanted an honest critique, so I pointed out several places that had mechanical writing problems (spelling errors, comma splices, mixed metaphors, grammar flaws). I also examined her table of contents and showed her how the organization of her book could be revamped and structured better.

The woman asked if I'd be willing to go through her entire 288-page manuscript and copyedit it, as well as make notes about how to restructure it. I said yes, and I handed her my rate sheet for editing work.

The woman flinched and said, "You expect me to pay you this much just to proofread my manuscript?" I pointed out to her that it would take me from five to ten hours to complete all the work required to correct her pages, and I explained that when I spent time on her project, I wouldn't be able to work on my own writing projects. I would need proper compensation.

"I think you're exaggerating the weaknesses in my book," she said. "I'm going to talk to some publishers at this conference and get other opinions."

I told her I felt that was a wise thing to do, although I knew she would get the same response from everyone she talked to.

At the end of the conference I saw this same woman waiting for a shuttle bus to the airport. I asked her how her meetings had gone.

She lifted her chin, sniffed, grimaced, and said, "I don't think any of those publishers have a clue as to how valuable my topic is. I'm going to show them what a mistake they've made in turning me down. I'm going to self-publish my book." And with that, she boarded the shuttle and rode off.

## Time Is a Hard Teacher

Two years later at another writers conference, that same woman approached me. She was emotionally broken. She told me she had gone home, signed a contract with a self-publisher, and had ordered five hundred copies of her book to be printed. She didn't hire an outside editor, feeling sure that the message of her book would make it a best-seller.

Instead, when the book came out, she became a laughingstock. Online reviewers made fun of the poor-quality writing. No one would hire her for speaking engagements, assuming that since she wrote so poorly, she must also speak very poorly. Not even her closest friends would pay her money for the book. She lost thousands of dollars, was publicly humiliated, and wound up with a garage full of books nobody wanted.

"I thought I was serving the Lord by bringing out a book that would help people," she told me. "But in my haste for success, I offered up a blemished lamb, and my sacrifice was unacceptable."

I wish I could say this was an isolated case, but that's not so. It occurs so frequently, I feel compelled to write about it. With self-publishing so prevalent today, would-be authors are trying to take shortcuts by rushing poor material into publication. But, as my good friend Jerry B. Jenkins is fond of saying, "There's a big difference between being *published* and just being *printed*." He's right. And, usually, that difference is in the quality of the book's content, presentation, research, organization, and overall writing.

## Seek the Right Editing

My advice to developing writers is to seek editing in stages. I've mentioned these points before, but they bear repeating.

First try to become part of an active writers club, where you can read your material aloud or pass it around for feedback. Maybe the other members won't be professional writers, but in all likelihood they will be voracious readers, and they can tell you if they found your manuscripts interesting, understandable, and readable. They can point out certain strengths you have, as well as flag some weaknesses not obvious to you.

Second, you can attend writers conferences at which you can submit sample pages of a work in progress and, for a slight fee, a competent instructor will edit your material and then display sample pages on an overhead screen. These "manuscript makeovers" or "thick-skinned critiques" will show you ways to improve your manuscript, as well as let you observe other students' writings and gain from the editing they receive too.

Third, when you are ready, you can hire a reputable copyeditor to go through your entire manuscript, marking it for grammar, syntax, punctuation, spelling, format, transitions, style, research, structure, logic, and content. Usually, by asking other writers you meet at writers conferences, you can get referrals and recommendations of copyeditors who have excellent reputations among writing circles.

Your goal will be two-fold. Not only will you want to have your manuscript professionally edited, but you will also want to work with someone who'll explain how you can avoid making the same mistakes in the future. For instance, here's one example of the personal notes I write to my editing clients: "You are creating split infinitives. Let me explain what they are and how to fix them."

Way back on September 1, 1980, *Time* magazine ran a four-page feature called, "The Decline of Editing." They showed how even the most elite writers of that day—Gay Talese, Bob Woodward, Judith Krantz, Alvin Toffler, Robert Ludlum—had released books with passages of pathetic writing because they thought they were too important to have anyone edit their material. The critics ripped them to shreds. Today, with self-publishing, the problem has only worsened.

Don't offer blemished lambs. You'll wind up being the one sacrificed.

## Support Team Tip 5
### Learning from a
### Master Editor

**Many readers, reviewers,** teachers, and critics complain today that no great works of literature are being created. The publishing world is so hyper-concerned about a writer's platform and sales potential, there is very little focus on quality writing and literary excellence.

Can this be changed? What was the magic element found in book publishing of the 1930s, '40s, and '50s that seems absent today? I believe numerous factors are involved, but chief among them is there are few editors who can recognize quality writing, can edit quality writing, and can find the time and energy to help quality writers reach their full creative maturity.

Maxwell Perkins (1884–1947) was probably the last of the master editors. Under his guidance and mentoring, works of stunning brilliance came forth from authors who were virtual nobodies until Perkins championed their talents and honed their skills. Ernest Hemingway, recipient of the Nobel Prize for Literature, was a protégé of Max Perkins. So was F. Scott Fitzgerald, whose book *The Great Gatsby* was voted "greatest novel of the twentieth century" by a consortium of two hundred fifty university professors surveyed by Modern Library. Perkins also established the careers of Marjorie Kinnan Rawlings (*The Yearling*), Thomas Wolfe (*You Can't Go Home Again*), James Jones (*From Here to Eternity*), and numerous historians, political essayists, humorists, theologians, and biographers.

Five key traits exhibited by Max Perkins made him what biographer A. Scott Berg has labeled an "editor of genius."

1. **Max Perkins could talk the talk of writing**. He also understood what made a book great. Perkins graduated from Harvard University with a degree in economics, but he had taken several courses in English from gifted professor Charles Copeland, himself a playwright and essayist. After graduation, Perkins was a general reporter for the *New York Times,* where he learned to write fast, accurately, and on deadline. He joined Charles Scribner and Sons Publishing in 1910 as an advertising manager, but his keen insights on how to promote authors' careers and sell books made Charles Scribner move Max directly into a position on the editorial board in 1914. Max stayed at that job for thirty-two years.

   Max's administrative assistant once wrote to a friend, "So many of his authors said that he could talk about literature better than any author." Indeed, Max was so widely read (he gave a copy of *War and Peace* to anyone who would accept it) that he instinctively knew what a book needed. He could explain those missing elements to an author in ways that were artistic, logical, and workable.

Often Max knew better than his authors what they should be working on and developing. After Marjorie Kinnan Rawlings had rather dismal sales with her first novel, *South Moon Under*, she was going to write a novel about an aristocratic Englishman. Max told her she should instead write a novel about the savage scrubland of Southern Florida, where people eked out a pioneer-like existence. Max wrote to Marjorie, "A book about a boy and the life of the scrub is the thing we want. It is those wonderful river trips and the hunting and the dogs and guns and the companionship of simple people." It took her three years to write it, but when Rawlings finished *The Yearling*, it won the Pulitzer Prize, became the best-selling book of 1938, and has never gone out of print.

2. **Max Perkins had vision and defied convention.** When Perkins first joined Scribner's editorial board, it had a reputation of being a conservative publishing house steeped in traditional tomes as produced by Sherwood Anderson, Sinclair Lewis, and Theodore Dreiser. Perkins aggressively sought new voices able to reflect distinctly American themes. He met with powerful resistance.

   For instance, when a manuscript by the then-unknown F. Scott Fitzgerald arrived, it was rejected by every editor except Max, who saw potential brilliance in the young author's style and delivery. Max fought until the company relented and released *This Side of Paradise* and then Fitzgerald's follow-up novel, *The Beautiful and the Damned*. Both were commercial failures, but Max continued to encourage Fitzgerald to write.

   Likewise, Max was so convinced that an unknown former newspaper reporter named Ernest Hemingway was destined for greatness, he actually purchased a terrible, very poorly written satirical novel by Hemingway just so he could get the rights to *The Sun Also Rises*.

3. **Max Perkins did whatever it took to get a book published.** When Thomas Wolfe showed up with a crate filled with

manuscript pages, Perkins worked with him an entire year before Wolfe's first novel, *Look Homeward, Angel,* was ready for publication. Perkins described it as "putting corsets on an elephant." Wolfe's second novel was over a million words long, and it took Perkins and Wolfe more than two years to separate it into two different novels.

4. **Max Perkins invested in authors, not just individual books.** F. Scott Fitzgerald had financial difficulties, a tumultuous marriage, drinking problems, fear of aging, poor health, and self-doubt. Perkins lent him money, wrote him letters of encouragement, and did all he could to make Fitzgerald feel competent and capable. Often Max would write from twelve to fifteen letters a day to his various authors, offering uplifting words and checking on the progress of their writing. Thomas Wolfe, who often fought with Max over scenes in his books yet bowed to his insightful literary wisdom, wrote in a letter to Perkins, "In all my life, until I met you, I never had a friend." To Perkins, his writers were artists, craftsmen, dreamers. He showed them respect.

5. **Max Perkins was a master of time management.** Max would work at his desk wearing his hat. If someone popped into his office for a chat, Max would say, "Oh, I was just on my way out," pointing to his hat, "but please stay for a minute or two and tell me how you've been." The person would stay only a few minutes and then leave, and then Max would return to his work. Every day he rode a train to and from work for nearly two hours each way, and he used that time to read and edit. He worked weeknights and weekends in order to hit deadlines. He came to meetings prepared, and he left as soon as possible. He was a man who cared about results.

Today's editors could benefit from emulating Maxwell Perkins. He was responsible for raising American literature to new levels. He netted great profits for his company by nurturing young writers who produced books that became classics and never went out of print. Truly, the life and editing strategies of Maxwell Perkins are worth studying, especially if we ever hope to return to the days of producing quality literature instead of mere disposable packaged books.

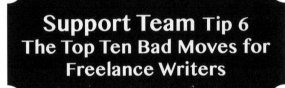

Support Team Tip 6
The Top Ten Bad Moves for
Freelance Writers

**Developing a solid** working relationship with editors is the lifeblood of a freelance writer's career. Offending editors or disappointing them is professional suicide. Make sure you don't sabotage that relationship and become *persona non grata* by committing these errors:

10. **Fail to do original research.** Editors themselves can do a patchwork job of splicing random quotes and statistics gleaned from the Internet. That's not what they want for articles. They want exclusive interviews with expert sources, reports on the latest research related to a topic, and a finished manuscript that is coordinated, fluid, and solidly on topic from start to finish.

9. **Fail to hit deadlines.** Jerry B. Jenkins notes, "When I was editor at *Moody Magazine*, ninety-nine out of one hundred writers failed to come in on or ahead of deadline. Those who did received additional work from me. Editors need writers they can count on to deliver the manuscripts on time."

8. **Refuse to accept editing.** I have been writing vignettes, fillers, and articles for *Evangel* for twenty years. The editor, Julie

Innes, often will make editing changes to my manuscripts. I never argue with her on these matters. She knows what she wants for her publication. As often as not, she improves whatever I've submitted to her. Writers who get defensive about being edited will alienate editors and lose opportunities for future writing assignments.

7. **Be redundant with ideas.** A writer's idea for an article might be appropriate for the publication being contacted, but if the editor has just published an article on that same topic in a recent issue, he or she will not want to repeat that information so soon. Study the back issues of a periodical. Send fresh ideas, new material, and original feature suggestions.

6. **Sidestep negative feedback.** Sometimes, after your article gets published, one of your sources will contact you and complain that you failed to mention the trophy he won in a golf tournament (even though the article was about Internet security), or someone will be upset because you mentioned her actual age. Referring these people to the editor is a cop-out. You need to deal with those issues and resolve these problems yourself. You chose those people to be your sources, so you are responsible for appeasing them.

5. **Double-dip with competitors.** If you promise an editor that you are giving exclusive rights to an article, make sure you stick to that agreement. Jim Watkins was once getting ready to go to press with an issue of *Vista* magazine when he discovered that another periodical had just published an article he thought he had bought exclusive rights to. He called the other magazine's editor and was told that the other editor thought he had bought exclusive rights, too. Needless to say, Jim killed the article in his publication, and neither he nor the other editor ever used the services of that freelancer again.

4. **Exceed the word count.** Some freelance writers fall in love with their own writing. They make the mistake of assuming the editor will appreciate the bonus verbiage. No,

that will never be the case. Read the publication's guidelines and strictly adhere to the word length for manuscripts.

3. **Adlib the specific assignment.** If you submit a query letter and get the go-ahead for an assignment, stick to that topic. Don't add anecdotes about funny incidents unrelated to the topic at hand. Don't tack on sidebars, reading lists, quizzes, or website recommendations if none of that was assigned in the original agreement. Stay focused. Deliver what you were assigned to write.

2. **Forget who is in charge.** John R. Ingrisano, former editor of *Sales Builder Magazine*, recalls, "Some freelance writers would try to tell me why their articles should be the cover stories or why I should not put ads on the pages where their features would be printed or why I should run photos of them with their articles. I politely but directly informed them that I was not a public relations flunky working for them. I made the decisions about how my magazine would be published."

1. **Fail to show appreciation.** If you have an ongoing relationship with an editor, it's appropriate to show some gratitude for that. I send Christmas cards to my editor friends and thank them for another great year of working together. I send complimentary e-mails to editors, praising them for making my articles look so great in print. When I see editors at writers conferences, I make it a point to shake hands, visit, and express appreciation for being able to write for their periodicals.

If you have ever opened your favorite magazines and wondered why the same writers seem to be published in issue after issue, it's a safe bet it's because they don't commit these mistakes. Now that you know what they are, don't you commit them either.

# Support Team Tip 7
## Ghostwriting
## Isn't Spooky

**There's no middle** ground. If you are a person's ghostwriter, that person will either hate you or love you. It's all about ego.

If the person whose name is going to appear on the cover actually wants people to think that he or she wrote the book, that person will want you to write a brilliant manuscript and then drop off the face of the earth so that he or she can go on radio and TV talk shows and take kudos for writing such a brilliant artistic masterpiece. (I actually had a client break into tears recalling how "emotionally gut-wrenching it was to write chapter nine." Oh…pul-eeese!)

So, let's put our cards on the table. Most ghostwriters, including me, do this for the money. Thus, rule one is to *charge plenty*. I mean it.

Let's get the negatives out of the way.

1.  **Ghosting causes a split personality**. The publisher is expecting the ghost to deliver one kind of book, but very often the client wants a totally different kind of book. When in doubt, favor the one paying you.

2.  **Ghosting is hard work, but often you get no credit for your labors**. One woman, whose entire book I wrote, thanked me on the acknowledgments page for "proofreading assistance and help with typing."

3.  **No matter how the book fares, you, the ghost, will come off the loser**. If the book hits number one and sells five million copies, you won't get a dime more than the work-for-hire flat rate you were originally paid. If the book tanks, everyone will blame you personally for producing an inferior manuscript.

By now you may be wondering why a guy like me, who has written more than forty-five books under his own name or pen name, would also have ghostwritten eighteen books for other people. One reason is because writing is what I do, and, as I've mentioned before, a bad day writing is better than a good day mopping floors at a fast-food restaurant.

Another reason is that sometimes the clients are really very nice people. For example, when I ghosted a book for Dr. Chris Thurman, a prominent psychologist in Texas, he turned over all of his notes, rough drafts, and research to me, and he also allowed me to follow him for five days, constantly taping interviews with him. The book I wrote, *The Truths We Must Believe* (Thomas Nelson, 1991), sold very well. It didn't carry my name anywhere, but in the book's preface, Dr. Thurman wrote, "I gave Dennis E. Hensley a lump of coal and he gave me back a diamond." That was gracious.

Most ghosting is by flat fee. A publisher will contact you and say that famous model Suzie Sweetsmile needs a book with her name on it. The advance will be $20,000 and it will all go to you (usually half in advance and half upon completion of the manuscript). If the book ever sells enough copies to work off that advance, all future earnings will go to Suzie. Some small publishers will pay only $6,000 for a ghosted project, whereas Charles Leerhsen was paid an estimated $150,000 to ghostwrite Donald Trump's book *Trump: Surviving at the Top*. But then, Mr. Leerhsen was a staff writer for *Newsweek,* and you (to quote Chevy Chase) are not.

Here's my suggestion. Listen first to what the editor offers, and, if you like the terms, accept the deal. If not, explain why you need more money, such as you've had better offers from other publishers or you could earn more money writing books under your own name.

Make a counter offer. If the editor agrees, close the deal. If she says it's too much, thank her for calling you, and go back to whatever you were writing that was paying you better.

Before you sign a ghosting contract, get three questions answered.

1. **What is the deadline?** If the book isn't needed for a year, you can work at a leisurely pace and do other assignments along the way. Thus, a 50 percent advance up front and 50 percent upon completion isn't a bad deal. However, if the book is needed in three months, it will consume all your time, so it's reasonable to ask for 75 percent of the advance up front so you'll have money to live on.

2. **Will there be an expense account?** This is crucial. If your source person is in California and you live in Kentucky, who is going to pay for the airfare for the interview trip? What about motel bills, rental cars, meals, photocopying expenses, mailing costs, and typist fees? You need to nail down how much will be coming out of your pocket so your entire payment won't be eaten up in research and operating expenses.

3. **What sort of recognition will the ghost receive?** Get it in writing. Will you be given no recognition? Will you get an "as told to" identification on the cover? Will you be listed as the book's coauthor? Will you be lauded on the acknowledgments page? Agree on this ahead of time.

You can become a working ghostwriter in several ways. If you know someone who is famous or is an expert in some area, try to convince that person to allow you to write his or her story and, thus, hitch your wagon to a star. Another option is to write directly for a client. Not all ghostwritten books need to be written for a publisher. Some individuals are prosperous enough to hire you directly to write their autobiographies or their specialty books. I placed an ad in a business magazine offering my services as a ghostwriter and wound up with three deals.

Try to get someone to recommend you. Networking is important. Have other writers refer you to their agents or publishers. Go to writers conferences and give your business card, résumé, and samples of your published works to editors and inform them that you do ghosting.

Work at being a topic expert. If you can become a writer who is an expert in a particular field (law, medicine, religion, the military), you can send your credentials to publishers who specialize in books in those fields, and you can line up ghosting assignments. In the late 1980s I started writing a lot of magazine articles about aspects of the insurance industry. I wound up ghosting books for leading agents and later even wrote four insurance-related books under my own name.

Obviously, ghosting is an avenue of revenue for writers. After one experience with it, you'll know if you have a ghost of a chance of surviving another go-round.

## Support Team Tip 8
## Create a Database of Experts

**After years of** working as a newspaper reporter while going to grad school, I took a job as chief information officer at a small, private college in northern Indiana. I was given a blunt mandate by the college president: "Put us on the map."

My predecessor had spent the previous five years sending out plain vanilla press releases about newly hired faculty, students on the dean's list, and elections for student government. What the campus needed was more energy, greater visibility, and elements of journalistic excitement. I had to figure out ways to lure reporters to campus so our students, faculty, and administrators could start getting in the public eye.

The solution I came up with turned out to be valuable for my writing career.

## Develop an Experts List

Having worked as a newshound, I knew the number-one challenge all reporters faced was coming up with fresh story ideas day after day. I roamed the campus, pushing my way into offices and classrooms, and asked everyone a series of questions:

- What are your areas of expertise?

- What have you published?

- Where have you made speeches, and what were your topics?

- What are your hobbies and avocations?

- What research are you currently working on?

I then made an alphabetical listing of twenty-six random topics and the expert who could be contacted to be interviewed on each topic. I began with "Apples: Dr. Diane Jenson, nutritionist" and ended with "Zoophobia: Prof. Glen McCloskey, psychologist." I sent copies of the list to all the regional newspapers, radio and TV stations, area magazines, and wire services. Phones started ringing, and our professors were soon showing up on the evening news and in the features sections of area publications.

Next, I prepared specialty lists of topics and experts. For example, I created a holiday hot-topics list that included such story ideas as "How the Bethlehem Star Was Formed, Dr. Dwight Berry, astronomer"; "Mastering Easter Egg Decorating, Prof. Linda

Zimmerman, artist"; and "Memorial Day: The Significance of Military Holidays, Dr. Alice de Graff, historian." Other specialty lists focused on health issues, family matters, financial planning, recreational activities, and world politics.

By the time I left that job four years later, enrollment had increased by 17 percent, three new buildings had been constructed on the campus, and alumni giving had risen 21 percent. I'm not saying I achieved this all by myself. But by putting the college "on the map" and keeping it there, I gave the school the stature, credibility, and status it so desperately needed in order to excel in other important areas.

## Building a List for Story Ideas

When I resigned from the college job in order to write full-time, I used that same game plan as a writer. I started to create vast lists of expert sources and interesting topics I could pitch to editors.

First, I contacted the president of our neighborhood association and asked if she would like me to prepare a monthly newsletter that would profile members of our association. I said I'd do it for $50 a month. She jumped at the chance. I started walking door to door, introducing myself as the newsletter editor and asking people about their jobs, hobbies, careers, trips, gardens, collections, famous friends or relatives, and memberships in clubs or service organizations. This tactic gave me lots of story leads.

Second, I followed a similar process at our new church, which had seven hundred members. I told the church administrative assistant I'd provide her with profiles of people she could print in the weekly church bulletin or put on the new-members bulletin boards. This move greatly expanded my sources of experts.

Third, I put together some sample scrapbooks (clip files) of my published articles and used them as credibility leverage whenever I needed to seek an expert source not already in my database. These articles helped me get access to unions, veterans' organizations, school boards, political campaign headquarters, and civic groups.

As I gained a reputation for having connections to people in all walks of life, I'd get regular calls from editors saying, "We need a piece on global population control by this weekend. Can you handle it?" And I'd say, "No problem. I know a guy." And almost always, I did, whether the topic was coin collecting, kayaking, drug rehab, the occult, or standup comedy.

Let me add here that a bonus feature of building a personal database of experts is that the experts will often refer you to other experts: coauthors, members of their professional organizations, students or teachers, fellow employees. It's like working with amoebae; they replicate themselves.

In feature writing, you don't have to be an expert on the topic you are writing about. You need only to have access to an expert. It costs you nothing, because everyone likes to see his or her name in print (Andy Warhol's "fifteen minutes of fame" concept). It also saves you time, since you can get all your statistics, data, anecdotes, and predictions from one prime source.

With computer spreadsheets and cross-referencing search engines, you can create your own source pool easily, adding to it continually. And because you will be talking with an actual person, you will get emotion, flavor, nuances, and assessments that you would never be able to glean from rows of statistics or dictionary definitions.

Which reminds me; if you need an expert on finding experts, I can help.

# Chapter 8
# Time, Money, and the Freelance Writer

**Time and Money Tip 1**
**Full-time Freelancing—It's**
**More than Manuscript Sales**

**If you are** thinking of quitting your day job and turning to freelance writing full-time, let me tell you the bad news and good news about that scenario.

The bad news: As a full-time freelancer you will never have paid time off for holidays or vacations; no one will match you dollar for dollar in retirement-fund contributions; your paychecks will not appear like clockwork every Friday; you won't have an expense account; you'll personally pay all premiums for life insurance and hospitalization benefits; there will be no office Christmas parties or year-end bonuses unless you provide them; and you won't be able to expect an automatic raise in pay just by remaining at your position for another year.

The good news: You won't be locked into a limited set salary; you'll have the chance to change people's lives through what you write; each assignment will be something new and challenging; often your work will involve travel; you'll meet interesting people as part of your research; and there's a good chance that a bit of prestige and fame might come your way.

Take a minute to reread those two paragraphs, and you'll notice something. Everything in the "good" paragraph relates to self-fulfillment. Everything in the "bad" paragraph relates to not running short of cash. In order to obtain the joys of the "good" paragraph, you have to learn to spend, invest, and use money properly. I worked as a full-time freelancer for fifteen years—some of them lean and some of them prosperous.

Here's what made full-time freelancing work for me.

## Create Passive Income

If you've set a goal to go into writing full-time in, say, five years, start now to create vehicles of passive income. Passive income is money you receive on a regular basis for doing nothing new. Writers need this because freelance income fluctuates in its amounts and arrives at erratic intervals.

You can begin in a small way by buying United States savings bonds on a regular basis. These bonds will earn interest for you every day. After one year, they become "liquid." In other words, you can cash them in at any time for whatever the accumulated interest would be up to that date. Thus, you win in two ways: (1) You will have a reserve pool of cash to fall back on in case of an emergency; and (2) if no emergency arises, your interest earnings will simply continue to compile on top of themselves.

Later, you can set up a brokerage account online and start to buy dividend-paying stocks and bonds. Some, such as certain utility stocks, will send you an earnings payment every month, whereas corporate bonds usually will pay you every three or six months. You won't have to do a thing except hold the stocks and bonds in your account, and the money will come in like clockwork.

You can eventually graduate to more aggressive investments for passive income. For example, after I had received some large advances on books, I put a down payment on a second home and turned it into a rental property. The rent covered the mortgage, taxes, and maintenance and also provided me with a small monthly profit. More importantly, however, was the fact that the renters were paying the house off for me, *and* the mortgage interest payments were providing nice tax deductions for me at the end of each year.

These last two points are of particular interest to full-time writers. Remember that you won't have a company pension when you retire; so, having a paid-off rental home or two that you can rent or sell for a nice fat profit will come in handy at age sixty-five. Also, those mortgage tax deductions will help because most magazine and book companies will send you a straight check with no taxes withheld, but at the end of the year you will be responsible for paying all of those taxes. Yikes! So, having some legitimate tax deductions to offset that income comes in handy.

## Creating Part-time Active Income

While passive income is wonderful, it can come in only after you've purchased the bonds or stocks or real estate. That requires cash. So does day-to-day living. As such, even while you're freelancing full-time, it is more realistic to establish secondary ways of generating cash flow.

Fortunately, numerous options exist. When I first began writing full-time, I also made myself available to substitute-teach three days a week. Later, I took on a part-time job as a stringer for a newspaper, writing two weekly columns, plus occasional feature stories. Other writers I've known have worked twenty hours per week in a library or bookstore. Some have done tutoring in their homes. One man I know writes newsletters for an insurance company twelve hours each week from his home office. Some writers sell Amway or Tupperware or Pampered Chef products. Until passive income has been built up to a substantial level, supplemental income will be needed.

## Leveraging Money

Many writers have access to pools of money they aren't even aware of. By discovering this money and leveraging it, they can generate additional income.

For instance, if you have owned a whole life insurance policy for ten years or more, it probably has built up cash equity. You can borrow this money from your insurance company. Because it is collateralized by the policy itself, the interest rate will be very low (somewhere between 4 percent and 8 percent usually, depending on when the policy was originally purchased). So, let's say you have a fourteen-year-old $50,000 whole life policy on yourself. If you borrowed $2,000 of the cash equity from the insurance company at 5 percent, it would cost you about $100 per year in interest. But if you turned around and invested that $2,000 into public utility stocks that paid you 7 percent interest, you'd clear $40 annual profit. This is called leveraging.

How aggressive you want to be at this is up to you. I took out a second mortgage on my home and invested the money I borrowed at a higher rate and kept "the spread." Let's say you are paying off a $250,000 home on a thirty-year mortgage. If you have $25,000 of equity in that home, you could easily borrow $10,000 on a second mortgage for about 6 percent (all tax deductible, I might add) and invest it in corporate bonds or utility stocks paying 8 percent. You'd have to pay some one-time closing costs up front, and there would be an estimated $600 of interest on the loan each year, but you'd be taking in $800 annually. Get it? Tax write-offs *plus* a $200 profit. That's leveraging.

If you then took your $300 profit and bought $600 of US savings bonds, you would be double-leveraging. You now are starting to understand the adage, "The rich get richer and the poor get poorer." It's because the rich know these techniques, but the poor do not.

## Paying Yourself Invisible Money

Another idea is to pay yourself money that cannot actually be seen. Although this money seems invisible, in time it will have a major impact on your financial stability.

Here's one example: If you own a home or condo and have a twenty-five year mortgage, you can save thousands of dollars by reducing interest payments to the bank. Mortgage payments are skewed so that at the front end of the loan you pay the most interest and the least amount of principal per payment.

In other words, if your monthly mortgage payment is $1,000, about $300 will go to reducing the principal and the other $700 will go into the banker's pocket as interest. That means that if each month you paid an extra $50 *directly against principal* (which you are allowed to do!), you would save about $216 of interest the banker could not charge you. Keep doing this, and your twenty-five-year mortgage will be reduced by eight years or more, and all the savings in interest would be *yours!* It's invisible in the sense that it never appears in your wallet, but it is very visible because it is money *that never leaves your wallet.*

## Overview

I do not wish to present myself as a certified public accountant, stockbroker, or lawyer. I'm not, and before engaging in these financial endeavors, you would be wise to consult with a trusted financial advisor. However, during my fifteen years as a full-time freelancer, these financial processes served me well.

In fact, you can bank on them.

## Time and Money Tip 2
### Make the Most of Your Writing Time

**I've written two** books on time management. The first one was by necessity. I was planning to leave my good-paying job at the end of the year in order to enter freelance writing full time.

I had a wife, two young children, and a house mortgage, so I needed to maximize my time in order to keep us afloat financially. I wound up being able to pull it off for a decade and a half before accepting a paycheck-job as a college professor. Let me share some tips on how to make the most of your available time for writing.

1. **Multitask with priorities.** Try to have at least three writing jobs going at the same time, but give the lion's share of time to the fastest-paying gigs. The key is to waste no working hours. I would first generate columns for newspapers and magazines that had me on retainer, because that was cash flow I could depend on. When those were caught up (I was always two months ahead in schedule, which editors loved), I would work on freelance feature articles. These took more time and were not always guaranteed sales—at least not right away— but when they did sell, they brought in more money than the columns and gave me greater national-byline exposure. Then, if my columns were done and I'd mailed out some features on speculation, I would work on my novel or a nonfiction book. If I needed to wait on research or to connect with a phone interview or I needed some down time to mull over a new scene in my novel, I would go back to writing columns or features. I never allowed any nonproductive time.

2. **Set a series of deadlines.** No matter what you are working on, whether an assignment from an editor or publisher or merely a project of your own choosing, set an ultimate deadline by which it must be done. Then break it into micro-deadlines. For example, I would say to myself that my nonfiction book of three-hundred manuscript pages had to be completed by October 15. Then I would back up to the current date, divide the number of weeks by the number of pages, and see that my micro-deadline had to be *one finished chapter of twenty typed pages per week*. Without deadlines, you are playing at writing. "Production equals profit," so you'll need to strive for closure on all writing projects.

3. **Follow a routine.** I used to write from 10:00 p.m. until 3:00 a.m. because my kids were asleep, the phone wasn't ringing, and no one was knocking on the door. Thankfully, my wife would get the kids up and off to school in the morning so that I could sleep in until 10:00 a.m. and then handle the mail, respond to phone calls, and do some reading until the kids got home from school. It was a crazy life, but it was regimented, and it was as though Daddy was working third shift. If you are writing only part time, it's still good to have a routine. Some people like to write from 5:00 to 7:00 a.m. before leaving for a 9:00 a.m. job. Some like to write in mid-afternoon when the youngsters are down for a nap. *When* doesn't matter. What does matter is maintaining continuity, productivity, and consistency.

4. **Track your progress, and give rewards.** I kept a production journal that logged how much I had completed on any given day. Sometimes I would get ahead of schedule, so I'd allow myself a nap or a midday movie with my wife or an outing with the kids. We all need incentives.

5. **Double your time by combining efforts.** In writing you can kill two birds with one stone. When I would come up with an idea for a nonfiction book, I would create a table of contents and then break each chapter into subunits. For example, in the earlier mentioned time-management book, one chapter was called "On-the-Spot Time Management." I broke it into four different articles I sold as columns or features: (1) time management at home, (2) in the car or plane, (3) at the office, and (4) while in client waiting rooms. This gave me cash flow, extra bylines, and eventually a completed chapter of my book.

6. **Take care of yourself.** The image of professional writers with a bottle of gin in one hand and a cigarette in the other is something out of Hollywood B movies. Writers need to exercise, eat properly, and get adequate sleep. Losing four days to a cold or the flu because your system got run down throws a monkey wrench into your productivity (and earnings). Along with this, I advocate mental and emotional health too. Time

for reading, church attendance, prayer, activities with friends and family members, and perhaps even some kind of hobby can be refreshing and rejuvenating. I enjoy playing the guitar.

7. **Think both short- and long-range.** At the start of your writing career, hustling to get bylines and bucks will seem like a rat race. Yes, you'll need to get your column in for Saturday's newspaper and finish that newsletter job for the neighborhood association. But create a game plan by which you can eventually put the time-consuming, small-paying jobs aside and work on better-paying opportunities, such as books and stage plays and scripts. By investing some time now into bigger projects, you'll eventually have passive income working for you (royalty checks, cash advances, excerpt sales, translation rights, movie options). This will take time pressure off you, as well as relieve financial strains.

Writing requires discipline. We can dedicate only so much time to it, so let's not waste a minute.

# Time and Money Tip 3
## Maximize Your Book-Writing Energies

**I teach at** a lot of writing conferences and workshops, and I meet a lot of writers. I don't care if a person is entering this field at age twenty-eight or seventy-eight; there is always a concern about making the best use of what time is available for writing. I get asked where a person should focus his or her writing energies. My response is that it isn't a matter of preferences; it's a matter of practicality.

Let's say a person is fifty and wants to become established as a working writer but also has dreams of one day completing some kind of *major* work of writing. The two aspirations seem contradictory, since it would probably take two years to write a five-hundred-page nonfiction book, edit it, revise it, and then start to market it. And then (gulp!) what if it doesn't sell? Yikes, what a waste of time!

My suggestion is to be more pragmatic. There's nothing wrong with wanting to write a book, but why stop all other goals in the process? Instead, write it progressively. First, create a table of contents that lists all the topics you want to cover in this book. Second, write each of those chapters as a separate feature article (or two articles, or an article with sidebars). Third, start selling the articles to magazines.

You'll accomplish three things at once:

1. You will begin to build a platform for yourself as a published expert on the topic of your book.

2. You will get byline exposure and also earn cash.

3. You will be writing your book.

This system has worked for me in writing more than a third of my published books. Try it! Use your time wisely.

---

## Time and Money Tip 4
## Recognize the Three Pitfalls of Literary Citizenship

**The hot catchphrase** in the world of publishing these days is "literary citizenship." In a nutshell, it is the premise that writers should be united in a self-sacrificing network of friends and helpers, all dedicated to advancing the careers—and lives—of fellow wordsmiths. On the surface this sounds like a noble goal and honorable cause, but as a person who has been in the writing profession for half a century, I see a lot of potential pitfalls for freelancers.

First, *don't confuse professional networking with social networking.* I am totally in favor of having a series of solid contacts with editors, accomplished authors, radio and TV talk show hosts, publishers, and literary agents. These people are the movers and shakers of our profession.

They're goal-oriented, experienced, connected, and productive. By working with them in a quid-pro-quo situation, they can help advance our careers as we, likewise, advance theirs. For example, if you refer a hot new writing talent to an agent or publisher and that leads to a contract, those folks will be very open to looking at *your* material, too. If you are willing to read the galleys of a pending book and provide an endorsement quotation for it, that author, in turn, will be open to reading the galleys of your next book and potentially offering an endorsement quotation for you. These are professional relationships.

Social networking, however, has the potential to drain writers. Sure, we're supposed to gain friends and followers who supposedly will plunk down money for our books and help with word-of-mouth advertising. But we *must* maintain a balance. It saps time when writers go on Facebook to read about a friend's baby who has cut her first tooth or about a retirement party that was held for a neighbor down the street. I literally have no time for needless chit-chat. I have looming deadlines, most self-imposed. I have open communication lines for people who are my close friends (most are in the publishing world in one way or the other) or business associates. The rest is clutter. That may seem cold, but it's just reality in the world of professional writing.

Second, *don't confuse craftsmen with leeches.* People involved in literary citizenship believe they have the right to send others their poorly written manuscripts and receive proofreading, editing, and insightful feedback. Instead of reading books on writing, attending writers conferences or college classes on writing, or being directly involved in a small-group critique circle, they want a shortcut. They want to find people to "fix up" their manuscripts so they can submit them for publication. When people like that approach me, I send them my editing rate sheet. Sometimes they are shocked that I would want substantial compensation for revising their material. But why would I want to pull myself off of my own writing projects in order to invest hours in the work of an amateur? Uh-uh. Writing for myself is hard enough.

This is not to say I am not open to exchanging manuscripts with fellow professionals. For example, my buddy John R. Ingrisano and I have been friends since we finished our master's degrees in college in 1973, and throughout the years we've bounced manuscripts off each other many times. I wrote the foreword for one of John's books, and he was my publisher for four of my business books released by R & R Newkirk in the 1980s. Recently, he sent me the opening chapters of his novel in progress, and I read them and wrote comments on the pages and sent them back within a couple of days. John will do the same for me someday. He's not a leech. He's a highly skilled craftsman. Know the difference.

Third, *don't confuse community with captivation.* Much of literary citizenship involves people who are writing in similar genres. They associate in public or online to a level of exclusivity. For example, at open-mike readings in coffeehouses and chat rooms strictly for poets, participants visit with each other, exchange poems, offer feedback about word choices or rhymes, and share reviews of poetry chapbooks they've recently read. If poetry is someone's passion and that person has no need to earn money as a writer, this may be a lot of fun. However, the world of publishing is no longer that narrow.

Today, with traditional publishing being supplemented by online publishing, indie publishing, print-on-demand books, and e-books, modern writers have to be authors, editors, publicists, agents, and publishers all by themselves. This just isn't possible by having a "social club" mentality about enhancing a writing career. Today's writers must explore new publishing options, attempt to write in a variety of genres, work with people in a vast array of publishing venues, and investigate professional networking options far afield.

I understand the value of a publishing house or literary agency having a large network of people who want to discover new releases or read about the lives of authors. I cooperate with that every time I have a new book come out. And I also know the value of maintaining a professional website (dochensley.com) for publicity purposes. Nevertheless, the idea that all writers are in a tribe or a hive working equally is both naïve and self-defeating. By necessity we must protect our time, maximize our resources, and sustain our creative energy.

Writing is and always has been a lonely profession. I understand why many new writers, not used to this alienation and solitude, might desire companionship. Fine. Just make it a fair relationship and exchange.

---

## Time and Money Tip 5
## Take the Free
## Out of Freelance Writing

**During a three-**month period, I was asked to help write a church-history book, a web page for my class reunion, a newsletter for the neighborhood association where I live, interviews for a publication supportive of a local charity, and an advertorial for a veterans' group. I said no each request. All of these jobs were going to be *pro bono*, and I can't take *pro bono* to the store and use it to buy milk and bread.

Outsiders to our profession think writing is fast and easy, that we have all the time in the world, and that seeing our names in print is enough payment to woo us. Lawyers, accountants, life coaches, psychiatrists, and fitness trainers charge for their advice and services. Writers must do likewise.

The most frequent question I hear in response to this is, "But how much should I charge?" The answer to that is easy. You charge slightly more than what you could earn by working for yourself.

Let's use real numbers. I have students at my college who are excellent at writing devotions. They can usually write, type, and submit a 175-word devotion in about an hour. Payment from *The Secret Place* or *The Word in Season* is $20 per devotion and from *The Upper Room* or *The Quiet Hour* is $30 per devotion. So, at an average of $25 per devotion, if a student spends four hours on a Saturday afternoon writing and submitting four devotions, she can make $100.

Thus, if someone says, "Can you write my company newsletter?" and the freelancer estimates it will take about three hours to put it together, the reply will be, "Yes, and my fee would be $85." She knows she can make $75 by writing on her own for three hours, plus she'll get byline visibility. So, she makes that amount her bid, plus $10 extra for forfeiting bylines. If the other person says that's too high, then the freelancer says thanks anyway and goes back to working for herself.

Now, obviously, no writer wants to spend the rest of his or her career writing only devotions or fillers for trade magazines or columns for the local newspaper or vignettes for Sunday school take-home papers, even though it may be steady work. Thus, there must be some trade-offs. And since, as writers, our most valuable commodity is our time, we have to prioritize it.

1. **Take time to expand markets.** Send out query letters, even though doing so is time-consuming. Finding new, better paying, higher visibility markets actually pays in the long run. Follow up on query letters, too. That is not being a nuisance; it is being professional. If that lead has nothing for you, you need to be able to move on to someplace or someone else.

2. **Beat deadlines.** If you want to gain more work and faster pay, then submit your assignments early. The sooner you can bill, the sooner you can get paid and ask for another assignment. Thus, don't stall. Get started immediately on any job that comes in. Generally speaking, freelance assignments always take longer than we estimate (phone calls or e-mails not returned, computer breakdowns, personal illness), so get to the research and writing promptly.

3. **Create a client base.** Grunt work, such as doing an insurance agency's monthly newsletter or updating a church's web page or writing a gardening column for the Sunday newspaper, may not be glamorous. But it creates cash flow. If you know that your core expenses will be met each week by repetitive writing assignments, you won't fret over investing your extra hours in exploring new markets, logging an afternoon working on your novel, or taking an evening course in pursuing your master's degree.

4. **Milk the material at hand.** Before switching to a new assignment, make sure you've maximized the sales potential of your current project. If you've written four devotions, can you add two anecdotes to each one and turn them into magazine features? Can you change the format and repackage the devotions as one-page radio devotional scripts? Can you assemble them as part of a thematic devotional book for college students, senior citizens, single moms, or members of the armed forces? Don't reinvent the wheel until you've put the whole car on the road.

5. **Voice your needs.** If you get offered a writing job from an editor, agent, or consulting client and you realize the job will entail travel, mailing costs, or other related expenses, say up front that you will need compensation for this overhead. It does you no good to earn a $500 payment if you've racked up $375 in meals, gasoline, envelopes and stamps, highway tolls, and the services of a transcriber.

6. **Match the market.** If you price your writing services too low, potential clients will wonder why your bid doesn't match the bids of the other two writers he contacted. Thus, you should check websites and ad brochures to find out what your competition is charging. Naturally, there are such considerations as your level of education, experience, and previous client references, but assuming most things are comparable, you should ask for what the market will sustain.

Scripture says that workers deserve their wages. In freelance writing, you, the worker, must decide what your wage should be. Don't sell yourself short. Writing is hard work, so you deserve proper compensation. Move from *free*lance to moderately-priced-lance to outright-expensive-lance.

❖

## Time and Money Tip 6
### How to Negotiate
### for Better Payments

**In 1969 when** I first entered the field of freelance writing, I was paid half a penny per word for short stories and articles that ran in Sunday school take-home papers or literary quarterlies. I remember once spending an entire Saturday and then four more hours on Sunday afternoon writing a 1,200-word comedy short story, on assignment, and getting a check for six bucks. Seeing my byline in print was exhilarating. Trying to make a living that way was impossible.

And if article payments were pathetic, book contracts were even worse. In those days some independent publishers were paying as little as a $250 advance on contracts that paid 3 percent royalties.

This was abuse, pure and simple, and it led to an eventual author revolt that gave way to the huge rise of literary agents now prevalent in all venues of publishing, as well as strong competition among major periodicals for the works of the leading writers. Unfortunately, the problem of proper author compensation has not been totally resolved. This is because of supply and demand. Literally thousands of novice writers are willing to sell their talents and services short just for a chance to break into print. Their logic is, "Yeah, I'm taking it on the chin now, but once I get established, I'll be able to earn higher fees." That only perpetuates the problem because, as they try to rise to new payment levels, they are replaced by other beginners willing to work for low wages.

So, how do you go about negotiating a better deal for article assignments or book contracts if you are not represented by a literary agent? It begins by going into any arrangement hoping to find a win-win outcome. Good relationships are not established by bullying, coercing, or strong-arming. Neither will deception, trickery, or deceit create a long-term bond. If both parties attempt to be empathetic to each other's needs, a level of trust can be established that can carry through to many additional working arrangements. During negotiation it's important for each party to understand the needs and limitations and expectations of the other party. Only then can specific deals turn out satisfactorily. A bonus is that the door will remain open for future assignments and deals.

When approached to take on a writing assignment, it is wise to thank the hiring party but to ask for some time to consider your needs. For example, people have come to me and said, "Our hospital (or social club or private school or mission organization) wants to self-publish a book about our fifty-year history. It will be given as a premium to those who are faithful donors to our work. We have earmarked \$_____ as payment for the writer. Would you be interested in accepting this assignment from us?"

At that point I need to determine the hours of research. Will I be given access to files, records, photos, and archival materials, or will I need to spend many weeks doing Internet research, conducting interviews with key people, and poring over materials in libraries? Also, how long do they want this book to be: a simple 75-page overview that they can print off as a folder with a plastic cover, or a 300-page in-depth history published as a trade paperback? Having calculated the hours required to do the job, the possible travel expenses (mileage, meals, overnight lodging), and the materials required (a full hard-copy printout of the manuscript? one flash drive containing the manuscript?), I then can come back and say whether the organization's budget is realistic or too low.

If the organization cannot increase the budget to meet your needs, maybe you can negotiate optional arrangements. For example, I was hired to write a book on the history of a hospital in Michigan that for fifty years has trained physicians for service in developing countries. When I went on-site for interviews or research, the hospital provided free lodging for me in a dorm used by doctors home on leave from foreign countries or back for additional training. I also was allowed to eat in the hospital's cafeteria for free. Additionally, the hospital assigned one of its administrative assistants to transcribe my tape recordings for me. We were able to cut expenses and meet both of our financial needs.

When discussing cost issues, it's important not to say anything that could be interpreted as defensive or aggressive. Be sincere, genuine, and transparent about your needs, and also try to figure out what may be behind the requests or parameters of the other person. For instance, I once was in an unpleasant negotiation with a person assigned to hire a writer to prepare a prospectus for the launch of a private school. This person considered me to be a "commercial writer," and when I asked what she meant by that, she said it was obvious I had a track record of writing for newspapers and magazines, but her project was about academia. When I shared with her that I held a PhD in English, she was stunned. She hadn't known that. Suddenly, her entire tone and attitude changed drastically, and we closed a deal. Often, it's knowing what is of key importance to the other party that leads to securing a contract.

I suggest using the word "we" when negotiating. If you say, "Can we look again at the expenses involved here?" or "Can we find ways to reframe the project to make it cost effective?" You will be engaging the other party to partner with you in finding ways to reach an agreement. However, at times you may need to say, "With other offers I now have pending…." or "Considering the fact that I gave you a discount on my last writing assignment...." This will use subtlety to make the point that you *can* walk away from this deal if it proves to be too costly for you to take on.

Writers need ready sources of income, so it is wise to keep existing clients happy. However, factors such as inflation, years of experience, and costs related to assignments justify asking for improved wages now and then. Don't be afraid to make your needs known. Just do it with tact.

# Chapter 9
# An Extrovert's Advice for Introverted Writers

**Extrovert's Tip 1**
**Leading the Discussion**
**Group—Yes, You!**

**Some people choose** a writing career because they believe they can work alone in a home office, isolated from the outside world, churning out words in blissful solitude.

Then—ack!—they get some success at it, and suddenly they're asked to lead an interactive seminar at a writers conference. Or they are invited to the national convention of the Romance Writers of America or Mystery Writers of America and are assigned to moderate a roundtable discussion. Or they get nominated to be their local writers club president, and they discover that every other meeting is a participatory feedback session led by the president.

If this is you, and if you haven't had a chance to spend the past five years attending meetings of Toastmasters International, let me provide you with some conversation stimulators that will allow you to initiate a group discussion and sustain it easily.

1. **Open the environment.** Rather than placing four rows of chairs to face you as the lecturer or emcee, circle the chairs so that participants will be looking at one another, ready to engage in an interchange of thoughts. Encourage them to bring along their cups of coffee, their electronic devices for note-taking, and any books or other support materials they feel might be appropriate for the pending discussion.

2. **Use prepared and spontaneous questions.** Ahead of time, create a list of specific questions you can use to initiate conversation. However, don't be afraid to explore tangents or sidetracks that participants may wish to ask about. After all, you're there to answer their questions and meet their needs. Spending five minutes on an ancillary topic won't derail the primary discussion, and it will validate the creativity and worth of the person who brought up the point.

3. **Adjust the questions and topics to the group's professional level.** Frequently I am asked to chair a forum for industry experts at the Write to Publish conference. To take part in this session, participants must be working agents, editors, or publishers or be authors with at least three published books. The questions I challenge this group with are high-level inquiries about publishing trends, developments in technology, social networking as it relates to global marketing, and the interfacing of mainstream and Christian publishing ventures. Conversely, when I'm teaching a class of eighteen-year-old first-year college students in an introductory course of professional writing at Taylor University, my questions include the topics of how the students are being influenced in their development as writers by the authors they're reading, what sorts of journal entries they've made that week, and what new web markets they are discovering for their manuscripts. Likewise, you will need to modify your questions to match the level of expertise of the group you are moderating.

4. **Pace your questions.** Never ask questions that can be responded to with *yes* or *no* or some other one-word reply.

Make the questions open-ended, seeking people's thoughts, opinions, ideas, and feelings. No one can give a one-word answer to, "How did you react to the ending of that short story?" or "What is your opinion about the use of violence in children's literature?" Once you ask your thought-provoking question, allow sufficient *wait time*. Give the person (perhaps the whole group) adequate moments to weigh what has been asked and then to formulate a wise and appropriate response. Be patient. Dead air isn't something to panic about.

5. **Involve the group in counterpoint questions.**
Often, as you are challenging the group with provocative questions, a participant will turn the tables and fire a question back at you, such as, "Sure, using the latest software for writing is a great suggestion, but what do I do, Terry, when my spouse doesn't think my writing income warrants more expenditures?" Instead of getting nervous about being challenged, use this as a way of engaging the whole group. Say, "Rickie has a good point. How do some of the rest of you cope with this situation?" This not only gets more people talking, but it usually also provides solutions to the problem being addressed.

6. **Use questions as previews of coming sessions.**
If your discussion times are recurring events, such as monthly writers club meetings, send out an e-mail or newsletter that will assist the participants in being better prepared ahead of time to engage in the discussion. You may say, for example, that at the next meeting the topic will be time management for writers, and each person should come in with questions related to goal-setting, writing-output quotas, multitasking, and balancing family and career (along with any solutions they might want to share). This will lift the preparation burden and will get the session started more quickly, since go-getters will be the first to volunteer to ask questions.

The more you lead discussion groups, the easier it becomes. Just keep in mind that you are there to help spread group knowledge among the participants while also being willing to offer your own personal experiences. It is productive chat time if you keep it focused and moving. Try it.

---

## Extrovert's Tip 2
## Speechwriting with Pizzazz

**Right before I** went on stage to deliver the keynote address at the 2013 Writing for the Soul conference in Colorado Springs, Jerry B. Jenkins stepped to the lectern to introduce me. Jerry smiled, then said, "I'm pleased to welcome my long-time friend, Doc Hensley, to the platform. If you've never heard this man speak before, let me give you a word of caution: *fasten your seatbelts!*" He then stepped back and waved me forward.

That humorous introduction pleased me, for it implied that whenever I give a speech, my listeners can be assured I'll be fast-paced, content-heavy, and entertaining. Too often, many orators today are *one* of these three, but not *all* of the three.

Denzel Washington, quoted in *Success* magazine ("Ties That Bind" by Mike Zimmerman, Oct. 8, 2012), said, "If it ain't on the page, it ain't on the stage." What he meant was, he couldn't be a great performer unless he first had a good script to work from. That's true.

180

Stand-up comics can be entertaining for an hour, but no one leaves their shows pondering heavy philosophical thoughts or meditating on ways to improve themselves or the world. A good speech must have a message that will impact listeners.

Crafting an impacting speech is a process.

1. **It has to have a central theme illustrated by a vibrant metaphor or a graphic story.** For example, in my speech titled "Submarine People," the central theme is that some people sink to depths of despair and failure in life, like a submarine with too much ballast. However, other people can jettison the ballast, rise to the surface, and move forward toward a worthy destination. Throughout that speech I return to the image of the submarine—sinking, resting on the bottom, blowing ballast, rising, cresting the surface, moving forward atop the waves. Listeners can envision the scene. They can relate to the metaphor. They can accept the challenge to get rid of the dead weight in their own lives and to rise to new levels. The image is not abstract; it's visual.

2. **Great speeches must have one or two phenomenal catchphrases.** You remember President Franklin D. Roosevelt's line, "The only thing we have to fear is fear itself." British Prime Minister Winston Churchill's line was, "I have nothing to offer but blood, toil, tears, and sweat." Julius Caesar said, "I came; I saw; I conquered." John F. Kennedy said, "Ask not what your country can do for you, ask what you can do for your country."[1] The challenge is to write a line so pithy, so succinct, so gripping, that it summarizes the entire point of the speech in a memorable, powerful, *quotable* phrase. In one

---

1. Astute readers will note the comma splice in this famous quote. We have chosen not to edit the error, because this is how it has appeared in print ever since John F. Kennedy first spoke these words during his inaugural address on January 20, 1961.

of my speeches back in 1996, I used the apostle Peter as an example of faith, and I said, "If you plan to walk on water, you first have to *get out of the boat!*" It was a simple statement, but I remember how the audience loved the challenge so much, everyone broke into applause right in the middle of my speech. Coincidentally, a few years later, John Ortberg came out with his popular book, *If You Want to Walk on Water, You've Got to Get Out of the Boat.*

3. **Create a detailed outline.** The audience needs to feel that the orator knows exactly where he or she is going with the talk. That means you have to start with a gripping story or statement or challenge (not some lame joke or a quote you borrowed from someone else). You have to have key points that flow systematically, logically, and fluidly, supported by clever anecdotes or insightful illustrations.

   You have to provide takeaway value so that the listeners don't dare go out for coffee refills lest they miss vital, crucial insights. Your transitions should be smooth, natural, and well-timed, perhaps by numbers ("...and secondly") or counterpoint words ("on the other hand...") or time triggers ("...yet even before this occurred..."). And you must have an ending that is not only conclusive but also clever and motivating. I close my submarine speech with this challenge: "This is your time. You're breaking free of the heavy waters. You're at the top. All hands on deck! *All hands on deck!*" (The audience always loves it.)

Once the speech is written, it must be rehearsed. Great orators are performers. I audio-record my practice sessions, listening for where I need to slow down, pause for effect, increase volume, and enunciate clearly. If I discover words that slur or echo one another or hit the ear awkwardly, I rewrite those passages. I practice in front of the mirror, testing hand gestures, head tilts, eyebrow lifts, shoulder hunches, sidesteps, and quizzical reactions. Body language speaks as loudly as do actual words.

One particular trick I use is to begin by speaking much too loudly for the first minute to overpower the audience. It becomes obvious that only one person in the room is now the center of attention, and it isn't anyone in the audience. Once control has been gained, I decrease volume and rely more on tempo, gesticulation, and articulation to hold everyone's attention. But starting strong is a key factor in successful speechmaking.

Today, when authors are expected to address writers conferences, appear on radio and TV talk shows, and record webinars and audio-blog entries on the Internet, becoming a skilled orator is a professional requirement. Get your start by speaking before attendees of clubs, conventions, retreats, churches, or schools.

What you say, who you say it to, and how you say it determine how effective your platform will be. So, write it like you say it, then say it as though you mean it.

# Extrovert's Tip 3
## Writing and Delivering the Dreaded After-Dinner Speech

**Having heard you** are a writer, people just *assume* you must also be a public speaker. So, you get asked to speak at the church's mother/daughter dinner or the men's weekend retreat or the couple's Valentine banquet. Go ahead, make them laugh and cry and sit wide-eyed in amazement at your wisdom. You've got twenty-five minutes.

1. **Develop a grid.** Break your speech into five sections. Create a grabber lead by using an amusing story, a reference to a current news event, or a tie-in with something related to the group you are addressing. In short, show you are prepared, don't stammer and stall, and get right into it. Next, work on your closing. You'll need to end with finality, such as stating a clever one-liner, sharing a heart-warming anecdote, or presenting a succinct summary of your key points. In between you will want some element of humor, some element of drama or serious contemplation, and then some element of application (the takeaway value).

2. **Localize your anecdotes.** Whether your presentation is one of humor or drama, if possible try to relate your jokes, illustrations, and references to the audience before you. For example, whenever I'm asked to do the closing banquet speech at a writers conference, I like to include motivational stories about writers who've succeeded by not giving up. I also like to share funny incidents that agents and editors have passed along to me about weird manuscripts they've been sent or odd requests they've received from authors. The wannabe writers in my audience can identify with half the stories and can laugh along with the others. Similarly, if you are speaking to your church's youth group, share some humorous recollections of back when you (and their parents) were in that same group. If it's a Red Hats meeting, make references to actual women in the audience who purposefully are wearing outrageous hats and then talk about mature women who have done great things in life. "Play to the audience" is a vaudeville term that applies here, too.

3. **Incorporate acting movements.** Rehearse your speech so that it sounds natural. If you tell an amusing story, pause for sufficient time to allow the audience a chance to enjoy the laugh. Don't rush ahead and step on your own comedy. Likewise, if you say an in-joke that this particular audience will understand, raise an eyebrow, nod your head, and wink at them. Let them know you're all in on the fun together. If you share something bizarre, ridiculous, or nutty, put a confused look

on your own face, indicating you don't get it either. Share the fun. In short, your body language, facial expressions, dramatic lulls, and other theatric gestures can make your presentation animated, participatory, and entertaining. No one wants to endure someone who stands rigidly at a podium, speaks in a monotone, makes no eye contact, and actually reads from a sheath of typed papers.

4. **Dress a step above the group.** Even costuming is part of your speech preparation. You need to make the audience understand that *you* are the focal point, that *you* are the one deserving its attention, and that *you* are the one with the message. Personally, I don't care if it is a writers club meeting, a post-dinner address to the Kiwanis Club, or even a gathering of high school students and their parents who are visiting the university campus where I teach, I wear a dress shirt and tie, sport coat, dress slacks, and shined shoes. You have to look the part if you want the audience to value what you will be saying. Never underestimate the impact of visual image.

5. **Don't clutter the talk.** Too often when people are not trained speechwriters, they try to pump up their limp writing by presenting a series of quotations from other people. Don't do that. One quoted reference—if that—is plenty. The audience came to hear what *you* have to say. Also, don't think you are going to impress people by rattling off lists of "startling statistics," because the human mind just cannot register abstract numbers. Don't tell us the percentages of children who were maimed or left starving or were killed due to poor working conditions during the Industrial Revolution. That won't impact us. Instead, if you tell us a tragic and moving story about one little boy named Oliver Twist, you'll hold us spellbound. We don't "get" numbers, but we do "get" people.

6. **Vary your method of delivery.** After-dinner speeches are not sermons or lectures. They are meant to be uplifting and entertaining presentations. Hey, these folks have labored all day and have just consumed a big meal. You're going to have to work in order to keep them awake and paying attention. As

such, keep your audience alert by presenting it with a range of stylistic engagements. Use exaggeration and understatement. Consider inserting some satire or irony. Drollness, absurdity, spoofs, wit, sarcasm, and even imitation will provide variety. You cannot surprise or thrill or excite an audience if the listeners tap into your delivery pattern and anticipate your punch lines. Don't let listeners figure you out. Force them to stay alert.

All of the above tips also work if someone approaches you and says, "I've been asked to give a speech at our company's retirement party this year" or "My parents are celebrating their golden anniversary and I'm supposed to give the post-banquet talk" and then they ask you to write the speech for them. Yep, same rules apply, except in that instance you're going to bill them.

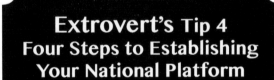

**Extrovert's Tip 4**
**Four Steps to Establishing**
**Your National Platform**

**I'm asked, "Why** do people such as television talk-show hosts and big-time basketball stars get published? They aren't even writers. I've worked on a manuscript for years, but can't get a publisher. What's with that?"

The answer? Visibility. Those people have platforms. Become known, and you too can attract interest from publishers. How? Bill yourself as an expert in your field and get out there, speaking on your topic.

186

## Start Small

Don't overlook obvious matters: business cards; brochures with your photo, a list of your speaking topics, and endorsements; a website promoting your writing and speaking.

Years ago I pitched a Saturday half-hour radio show called, "Freelance Writing Made Easy." I lined up two bookstores with fifteen-week contracts to underwrite the show. After a year I was so busy with speaking engagements, I ended the program and went on the road.

Contact independent TV outlets; create your own promotional blog; speak to public service groups (Kiwanis, Lions, Elks); speak at banquets, retreats, or teach night-school courses. At first, you may have to do some of this *pro bono*. Later you can charge a fee, as well as set up your book-sale table.

## The Success Factor

None of this prep work amounts to anything unless your presentations are stunning. Your next two bookings are sitting in each audience. When you knock a crowd for a loop, people talk. Nothing will boost your career as much as positive word of mouth. Never allow yourself to give anything less than a phenomenal presentation.

Each year I meet dozens of people who hand me a business card that says Susan Smiley, author/speaker. They've taken a three-day crash course in how to dress for success and prepare a speech. They land a gig or two at a ladies luncheon or PTA meeting. But their phone doesn't ring off the hook thereafter. There was no pizzazz in their presentation. All the promotional trappings were in place, but no one got excited about the speaker.

## Prepare and Deliver

Write a content-heavy, highly entertaining speech. Rehearse it, hone it, revise it until it's a knockout. Then, prepare another one.

If you are a great orator, you'll be booked at bigger venues. That leads to large, on-the-spot book sales and additional speaking engagements.

A big platform results in lots of books sold—and publishers love that.

**Business people today** are very conscious of the fact that they need to have a media presence. Most executives are connected to Twitter, Facebook, Linkedin, Instagram, and numerous other online social networks. However, this should not negate the continuance of more traditional methods of networking. Consider, for example, ways to make connections at conferences and conventions.

One lesson that online social networking has taught us is this: a straight advertisement will not generate sales. Instead, what attracts people to blogs or websites is the promise of help or advice. This, in time, wins social-media friends and followers who, in the long run, are prone to buy the blog-writer's book or service or seminar or product.

So, how do you "friend" someone at a convention or conference? Begin by being aggressive in meeting people. If you see someone standing alone, that person is new or shy or alienated. Befriend him or her, and you'll be amazed at the gratitude the person expresses. No one goes to a convention or conference with a desire to be ignored. Nevertheless, many high-tech geeks lack people skills. If you make the effort to connect with folks, you'll rapidly expand your networks.

The easiest way to draw a stranger into a conversation is to ask pointed questions, such as:

1.  What publishing house or literary agency or writers group do you work for or are active in, and what, specifically, do you do there?

2.  What range of products and services does your company/agency/publishing house offer, and what new ways will you be expanding in the coming years?

3.  How can I help you meet the folks you most need to connect with at this convention/conference?

Take the person's card. On the back of it, write notes concerning what the two of you talked about. Hand over your own card. If possible, do what you can to provide a free service, i.e., introduce people to each other who have a common area of need. Introduce newcomers to the officers of your writers club or professional organization (Science Fiction and Fantasy Writers of America, Society of Authors Representatives, Mystery Writers of America, etc.). Set up a lunch or dinner social time where new friendships can be established. Volunteer to attend speeches, demonstrations, or seminars these people may be part of.

After the conference or convention, do follow-up work. Make a phone call, send an e-mail, or drop a letter. Make it obvious that you were genuine in wanting to continue to be of service to each new contact. In time, you'll be able to share your catalogs, website links, and other business connections with these folks.

Internet links are usually generic, whereas a pat on the back is personal. Media contacts are mass-oriented, but the exchange of business cards is mutually gratifying. Online networking is done at arm's length, whereas engaging in conversation is up-close and intimate.

There is no denying that online social networking has its place in contemporary marketing. However, you cannot shake hands via computer. The need for personal, individualized attention will always exist, and you will benefit in numerous ways by meeting that need.

# Chapter 10
# Be Your Own Best Publicist

## Best Publicist Tip 1
### Becoming an Author-preneur

**Something weird happened** at a major writers conference where a book contract and a check for $20,000 were going to be given to a contest winner during the opening session. Although I had been one of the two judges who had narrowed the list of 187 competitors to five finalists, even I didn't know who would receive the first prize.

However, I was confident it had to be one of two particular novels I was incredibly impressed with. I had rated both books ninety-five out of a possible one hundred total points for character development, plot concept, writing mechanics, format and style, and thematic message. The other judge, if she agreed with me, would make one of these two books the winner, depending on how she might tip the scales.

When the winner was announced, the author went forward and accepted his contract, his check, and even a mock-up of what his book's cover would look like. Indeed, he was one of the two authors I had chosen as being worthy of the grand prize.

However, here's where it gets bizarre. Two days later I cornered the other writer, the one I felt had written an equally excellent book. I said, "I've been so busy teaching at this conference, I haven't had a chance to compliment you on the superb novel you wrote. No doubt, since you're one of the five finalists, several of the publishers and literary agents here this week have rushed to you with offers of representation or contract deals."

The writer shrugged and shook his head. "No," he said, "nothing like that has happened so far. I've been setting up appointments, trying to pitch my novel, but as yet I've had no firm offers."

This truly amazed me. From my perspective, his being one of the five finalists in a contest that awarded a twenty-grand contract would seem to indicate, "Here is a manuscript worth grabbing." But that hadn't proven to be the case, and I wanted to know why.

### Are You a Nobody?

So later that day, at a staff-and-faculty-only networking party, I approached several editors from major publishing houses and asked them pointblank why they weren't in hot pursuit of the novels by the four runners-up. The answers I received were almost identical, right down the line.

"We're realists at my company," one veteran editor told me as she toyed with her salad. "Having a publishing house underwrite a big contest like this is a draw. It attracts a lot of people to attend this conference, and it generates a lot of publicity for the sponsoring publisher. But the truth of the situation is, the people who enter contests like this are *nobodies*. They've published no previous books, they're not on the talk-show circuit, and most of them lead pretty dull lives. Turning them into celebrity authors would take us years. And even then, who knows if they would be capable of producing a second book of high quality.

"So, for now, we're sticking with writers who have an established platform. You know…high visibility and a proven track record in publishing."

I suppose this should not have come as a total shock to me. Selling my most recent book had included proving that I had a vibrant website, was booked for several speaking engagements at writers conferences and business venues in the coming year, and had contacts with several radio and TV talk shows where I would be welcomed to discuss my new book. Unlike the old days when my manuscript was all that really mattered, now current publishers were focused on my total package as a writer and celebrity. I, like everyone else, needed to prove I had brand identity.

## Talent Isn't Enough

"Aren't you taking risks?" I asked one editor. "Don't you want to discover new talent?"

He nodded and said, "Well, sure, we want to discover new talent. But, no, we don't want to take many risks. As such, we keep a close eye on small publishers and regional presses. If they find a writer whose books begin to capture a reading audience, then we swoop in and offer a better package and steal that author away. We've had no up-front gamble by doing that."

Another seasoned editor told me, "Twenty years ago I would scour magazines, searching for good writers who had clever ideas. If I saw a fascinating article written by a solid writer, I'd contact that person and suggest we talk about a possible book project. Well, today there aren't many major print magazines around, but I am doing the same thing with people's blogs. If I discover a talented writer who has created a large following, I see gold in that situation. I can help the writer formulate a book, and we can tap into his or her established following. Authors such as Seth Godin have proven it's a workable system."

Another editor told me, "We've become vicious at our house about quickly assessing a book's potential, which, of course, impacts a writer's future. We published a book recently that we felt had legs. We'd given the writer a nice advance and had planned a series of book signings, media interviews, and social-networking events. However, at the end of the first month after the book's release, we saw that the reviews were lukewarm and sales were sluggish. So, we cut our losses. We canceled the second run of the book, ended the media events, and informed the writer we would not be exercising our option to buy her next book. That's how fast things are determined in publishing these days."

## Enter the Author-preneur

What we can glean from blunt responses by the gatekeepers at key publishing houses is that today's writer has to be an author who is an entrepreneur. It's not enough to write a quality manuscript, although that is still important.

Today, the book author must also be a *marketing guru* (lining up webinars, podcasts, e-mail blitzes, network connections); a *multimedia expressionist* (writing blogs, establishing websites, booking talk-show appearances); *business opportunist* (selling book excerpts, setting up lectures or seminars or workshops); and a *personal publicist* (seeking endorsements for the book, getting profiles published in alumni magazines, hometown newspapers, sorority publications, and professional organization newsletters).

Much of the work that used to fall to the publishers has been transferred to the author. It's no longer a turnkey operation. It's a tourniquet operation, i.e., keep the lifeline of the book flowing, or the publisher will choke you off.

But how does one begin? Here are four ways:

1. **What you don't know, learn.** If you have no insights regarding social media, ask your kids or grandkids to teach you how to get wired. If you don't know how to build a platform, go to writers conferences where experts are on faculty, and attend their sessions. Take notes and adopt their systems.

2. **Make a list of your favorite writers.** Then go to their websites and see how they are promoting themselves and their writing. Adapt and borrow ideas from people who are succeeding at what you wish to be doing.

194

3. **Consider all publishing options.** Don't lock yourself into seeking only a standard print book. Evaluate the possibility of e-books, audio books, or even graphic novels.

4. **Think smaller.** Since the big houses are scouting the releases of smaller houses, be open to contacting university presses, regional publishers, and specialty houses. Get published. You cannot grow until you are at least planted.

Today's writer is not an extension of a publishing house; he or she is a partner with it. The sooner we all get up to speed on that, the sooner we'll accept our new roles as author-preneurs.

**Best Publicist Tip 2**
**Mastering the**
**FIfteen-Minute Book Pitch**

**Pop artist Andy** Warhol once said that every person, sooner or later, enjoys fifteen minutes of fame. In the arena of pitching book proposals, it comes down to fifteen minutes of fame or fifteen minutes of shame. When you attend a writers conference and schedule an appointment with a literary agent or book editor, you have fifteen minutes—sometimes less—to convince that person your book is worth considering for publication and that you are someone this individual will want to do business with.

That's not much time, so let's talk about how to make those minutes count.

1. **Look professional.** Although writers conferences are usually casual in attire, trying to convince someone to invest more than $35,000 to launch your book is big business. You need to look like someone who would appear impressive on talk shows, when giving speeches, and when meeting folks at autograph parties. First impressions are lasting ones.

2. **Have an actual book idea.** Some would-be writers come up with a great title and even some clever research, but trained editors can see what would make a good article and what would actually sustain a full book. A published book usually is somewhere around two-hundred pages, with about four hundred words per page, which is 80,000 words. Thus, if you don't have an idea that can be content heavy for 320 double-spaced manuscript pages, don't waste the editor's time.

3. **Know the competition.** Anticipate that the agent or editor will ask you what else is on the market similar to your topic. It's good that other books exist on your topic, because they show that other publishers have seen market value for it. Your job will be to explain how your book is different. Perhaps you have newer research, better photos or other graphics, a broader range of topics, exclusive interviews, distinctive sidebars or reading lists or quizzes. Emphasize how your book is unique and better than the competition. One special insider tip is this: Prove that your book will still be interesting a year from now when it finally gets into print and how it will contain enduring elements that will make it stay in print several years thereafter.

4. **Speak as though this person is a committee.** Although you are addressing just one person, he or she will have to champion your book before a publication board. It will be made up of people from sales, publicity, layout and design, marketing, accounting, legal, and editorial departments. As

such, explain how you will help to market the book via speaking engagements, blogging, social networking, library appearances, webinars, professional organizations, public readings, writers workshops, reviews, and autograph parties. Don't give anyone on the board a reason to reject you.

5. **Sell yourself with wild abandon.** No one likes a braggart, but when it comes to selling a book, you need to prove that you know what you're talking about. You can do this by providing a résumé that stresses your education, your list of previous publications, any honors or awards you've received, and your professional credentials. Stress the research you conducted in preparing this book manuscript. Additionally, if you can produce a list of endorsements from people with name recognition, this will certainly work in your favor.

6. **Hand over a solid book proposal.** Despite the fact that you will have a well-organized, extremely focused conversation with this agent or editor, you still will need to have a high-quality book proposal to leave with this person if he or she decides your book idea warrants publication consideration. Your cover letter will explain why you feel this publisher is right for your book; highlights of your career after age twenty; a terse description of your book ("*The Help* is about African-American maids who find ways to shame their oppressive suburban white employers during the 1960s"); mention of your best endorsements; and a word about your target readership. You'll need to have from one to three fully completed chapters, a one-page biography (write about yourself in the third person), a table of contents that you may wish to expand into an outline, a one- or two-page synopsis of the entire book (yes, do tell the ending), and information about your personal platform.

7. **Anticipate blunt objections or questions.** Editors may ask if the manuscript is "clean," meaning void of mechanical writing errors. Say (truthfully) that you've had other eyes go over the entire book (professional editors or maybe members

of your writers critique group). Editors may ask "Who cares?" about your topic. Have statistics ready, audience surveys, sales records of similar books. The editor may ask, "But who are you?" so have credentials *and experience* to show you are the perfect person to write and promote this book.

Contrary to common belief, editors come to writers conferences because they *want* to discover talented writers, and they *want* to find publishable books. How else can they stay in business? However, their greatest joy is to discover someone who is polished, professional, and savvy about writing and marketing books. This could mean a long-term working relationship.

So, when the clock starts ticking, use every second to show that you came prepared to do business.

## Best Publicist Tip 3
## Against All Odds:
## Believing in Your Manuscript

**Editors at book** publishing houses are always saying, "Show me something new, something different, something special, something unique," yet when I did, none of them liked it.

Don't get me wrong, I'd had plenty of success as a writer. At that point more than fifty of my books had been published, as well as some three thousand newspaper and magazine articles. Nevertheless, after spending three years creating a new genre I called the *fact-vella*, I found myself running into stone walls. No one I showed it to "got it," so no one wanted to publish it. The ordeal was depressing.

Here was my original idea: Everyone seemed to like motivational books that had lots of good content on how to succeed in life, but they also enjoyed stories. That's why a book such as *The One Minute Manager* had succeeded as a modern teaching parable (a story), yet *The Tipping Point* had succeeded as a statistical research book (content-heavy material). So, I thought that if I wrote a factual book with a novella embedded within it, I'd have the best of both formats. And, thus, I created the factual-book/novella, or *fact-vella*, as I began calling it. I thought it was entertaining, insightful, witty, and educational. The editors I showed it to thought differently.

"This is a hodge-podge," one editor told me after reading the first three chapters and the three inserted vignettes of the novella. "If you want to write a novel, do so. If you want to write a nonfiction motivational book, then keep your focus on that." This was especially painful for me to hear because I'd had five books published with the company this editor worked for, so I thought that surely my brilliant new idea would be welcomed with open arms. Uh...not so.

Another editor kept the manuscript for a week, then called me and said, "Hey, these fictional inserts are clever. They teach by example without being heavy handed. Why don't you pull them out, spend the next year expanding all of them, and then send this thing back to me as a completed novel? I'd be glad to consider it again." I groaned audibly and hung up.

Another editor went the opposite direction. She suggested, "Take out all of these silly little fictional diversions and, instead, add in a whole series of study questions, reading lists, quizzes, and sidebars with statistics, and turn this into a standard textbook. We might be able to market something like that." I wanted to pull out my hair.

Time and again I would reread my manuscript, and time and again I would tell myself, "This works! It's a fun way to learn. It's fast-paced, contemporary, and original. Why doesn't anyone like it?" Within four months I had racked up rejections from ten publishing houses, both large and small. The editors kept telling me that I had something "in there somewhere," but they thought that my mishmash-conglomeration of fiction and nonfiction was confusing instead of enlightening.

In a fit of feeling like a loser—like someone who had invested three years in a project that had no merit whatsoever—I poured my heart out to my wife. "If ten editors all saw fit to reject my book, I probably need to face the fact that it's a dud, not fit for publication."

My wife said, "Maybe that's why they're editors and not authors."

I looked at her a moment, then asked, "What do you mean by that?"

She shrugged and responded, "Well, you're an author. You focus on providing a product that you know readers will enjoy, something they'll find helpful and also entertaining. Your entire effort is concentrated on winning the approval of the readers. Editors, however, are locked in on trusting what has worked in the past. They fear risk. They prefer tried-and-true formats, standard messages, and traditional writing styles. If you plan to sell a book that'll be breaking new ground, you're going to have to find an editor who is—or has been—a successful writer, too."

In an instant it hit me that she was right. My writing wasn't bad. My *marketing* was. Immediately, I got on the phone with a long-time friend of mine, Jerry "Chip" MacGregor, a former acquisitions editor with Time-Warner Book Division and currently a highly successful literary agent. Chip himself is the author of more than twenty-five books. I explained about the book I had written and told him I needed to get the manuscript into the hands of some editors who had been on the other side of the desk, editors who knew about creative writing, not just copyediting and ad campaigns. Chip told me to send him the book, and he'd take a look at it.

Within forty-eight hours, Chip got back to me, telling me that the book had made him laugh, nod in agreement, and pause frequently to reflect. He loved it and said he would take me on as a client and the book on as a project. Chip made a list of editors in New York, Nashville, Chicago, Colorado Springs, and Los Angeles whom he knew to be more than number crunchers. These people were well-read. They were published writers themselves. And they had been in the world of publishing long enough to recognize the difference between a flash-in-the-pan whimsical idea and something that truly was groundbreaking and innovative.

Two weeks after sending out my manuscript, Chip started getting calls. Contract offers started to come in, including very respectable cash advances. Four publishers in particular entered into a bidding match, aggressively seeking the manuscript. In time, Chip called me and made a suggestion as to which editor and company he felt we should go with. It was Rick Steele at AMG Publishers, and I agreed. I signed the contract, and my book *Jesus in the 9 to 5* became slated for global release in the winter of 2013.

I learned three good lessons from this experience:

1. Each book will have to be judged on its own merit, so don't assume that your past track record will make publication of your next book a shoo-in. Do your best writing every time.

2. Pot-shot marketing is not effective marketing. These days, it's better to concentrate on contacting the editors and the publishing houses that seem most empathetic and aligned with your themes, your style of writing, and your reading audience.

3. At times you will just have to maintain faith in your manuscript even when no one else seems to appreciate it or enjoy it—much less "get it."

Stay focused on the readers, giving them what they want and need. If you do that, and do it well, sooner or later you *will* become a published writer. Meanwhile, go out and buy my newest book. I want to get a bigger advance for the series.

<hr>

## Best Publicist Tip 4
### Selling Your Book in Descending Sound Bites

**Remember when you** were a kid and enjoyed playing pirate with a toy telescope? Eventually you would turn it around, look through the wide end, and see all of the distant objects reduced to very small sizes. That, my friend, is what the twenty-first-century world of pitching books has become. I speak from experience, for in working with my various book publicists, I've had to condense the essence of my manuscripts so tightly, each description has gone from an elephant to an ant in four simple steps.

Here's what is going on. Publishers still need authors to help come up with excellent back-cover copy. After all, who knows the book better than its author? Additionally, however, the author now has to provide even shorter promotional copy for use in paid advertisements or blog sidebars or website promotional listings. Furthermore, the author has to be able to reduce the entire book to one paragraph for use in online reviews, e-mail blasts by the publisher, and newsletter inserts for book groups and writers clubs. Most difficult of all, the author must summarize the whole book in no more than 140 characters to send as a tweet.

My publicists coached me on how to write very tight promotional copy. I was told to imagine I was a potential reader trolling the Internet in search of something good to read. What about my book would set it apart from all the other books being promoted to the reader? How could I summarize it in a way that would pique the interest of a reader? How could I woo the reader without having to reveal too much content? Also, if someone had just finished reading my book and wanted to tweet a friend about it, what did I think would be the book's most exciting aspect to talk about in one sentence?

Naturally, in the longest of the promo-copy four versions, you can delve into specific key elements of the book's content. If it's a novel, you can mention the setting, the era, the major plot conflict, and the central characters. If it is nonfiction, you can refer to teaching points, target lessons, and insightful knowledge. As you write in more constricted venues, you will have to prioritize the most important elements and discard lesser factors. It's painful, but it helps if you think of it as a metaphor: present the bull's eye, not the entire target.

When it comes to creating the tweet, I can share a tip my pal Larry Weedon taught me when he was an acquisitions editor with Thomas Nelson publishers. He told me the best way to summarize a book in one sentence was to imagine it was like a movie being described in a TV listing. For example, Tom Clancy's *The Hunt for Red October* could be encapsulated as, "Russian nuclear submarine captain defects to America, bringing his submarine." That is so enticing, an audience would be won over instantly.

The next few pages show you how my book, *Jesus in the 9 to 5*, went through this shrinking process from back-cover copy to a single tweet. Even if your book has not yet been accepted for publication, going through this writing exercise will help you when you pitch it to agents and editors. You'll be four steps ahead in the eventual process.

# Four Versions of Promoting the Same Book

## Long Version
### (back-cover copy)
*Jesus in the 9 to 5*

## Synopsis

Would you be delighted if, upon pulling into the parking lot of your place of employment each day, you knew you would walk inside and work shoulder to shoulder with Jesus Christ? Or, would it be overwhelmingly intimidating to be working for someone who knew your every thought, your every move, your every ambition?

Such is the situation in *Jesus in the 9 to 5*, wherein motivational speaker and author Dr. Dennis E. Hensley actually allows you to step into a twenty-first-century company being run on a day-to-day basis by none other than Jesus Christ, himself. You'll be there as Jesus hires new personnel, establishes company training, and sets a quality-control system in place. You'll observe as Jesus is asked to judge a matter of employee theft, is defied by his employees about business management practices, and is forced to make plans to hand over his business because of his pending departure.

Along with the scenario of Jesus running a company, this book also provides insightful chapters on life-management skills as drawn from the teachings and actions of Jesus. You'll be shown how to improve your time-management practices, your communication abilities, your goal-setting and long-range-planning skills, and even your sales and outreach talents.

With wit, wisdom, and continuous momentum, this book reveals specific ways in which you can enrich your life, expand your personal and business horizons, and add new vitality in reaching your goals and aims in life. It's also just a lot of fun to observe Jesus in action as the director of a contemporary business operation.

So, clock in. Your first day on the job with Jesus is set to get started.

## 50-Word Version
## (online book reviews, newsletter inserts, blog attachments)

With razor-sharp wit, penetrating wisdom, and fast-paced teaching, *Jesus in the 9 to 5* not only reveals the lessons Jesus provided on how to manage life and business, it also lets readers see Jesus in action, running a twenty-first-century company on a day-to-day basis.

## 25-Word Version

## (e-mail blasts)

You've made Jesus the Lord of your life. Now, make him the boss of your company. Turn the pages and see how Jesus would manage a twenty-first-century business.

## 10-Word Version
## (58-character tweet)

Open this book and become a twenty-first-century employee of Jesus.

## Best Publicist Tip 5
### Don't Squander
### Your Money on Fads

**I speak at** a lot of writers conferences. Beginning writers constantly ask me if they should spend money on sure-fire programs that promise to make their books best-sellers. Let me give you my take on some of these promotional options, keeping in mind you will find other people who have very differing opinions.

1. **Book-Proposal Listing Services.** I know of at least seven organizations that charge between $75 and $200 to list your book proposal on their websites. They each claim that editors and publishers are constantly scanning these proposals in search of new talent and undiscovered masterpieces. For six months while on the speaking circuit, I asked every editor and literary agent I worked with if they ever turned to these lists. The uniform answer was, "Are you kidding? I'm already so backlogged with unread manuscripts, why would I go looking for more work? No, I never look at those websites."

   These websites appear to be legitimate. They claim they will not list books that are not of "professional quality." (Some of these organizations will offer to help bring the manuscript up to professional quality for a steep editing fee.) However, I have scanned some of the offerings. Indeed, some have well-written proposals and sample chapters, but many others are downright pathetic and have no chance of ever getting published. This leads me to believe that if you'll pay the access fee, you'll be welcomed aboard. My judgment therefore is, *avoid these marketing services.*

2. **Book Trailers.** For decades movie theaters have run "movie trailers" (previews of upcoming films) to create interest in new films. In 2007 some web designers started doing the same thing for new books. Today, thousands of book trailers can be seen on social-media sites and personal blogs.

Originally, the idea was that book salespersons would carry a laptop into a bookstore, run a two-minute book trailer for the store owner, and generate enough interest to secure a big order. However, the cost of the book trailer was billed directly to the author, usually at $1,000 or more. That meant the author had to sell at least two-thousand copies of a $5.95 paperback book just to pay for the book trailer. Sometimes it worked, as when Chad Kultgen's first novel, *The Average American Male,* sold 26,875 copies in hardbound after a million and a half people viewed his book trailer on YouTube. However, more often than not, book trailers have not been successful in selling books.

The problems with book trailers are numerous: far too many of them exist, many are done in very amateurish ways, and the professional ones cost big bucks. Where they have become effective is when writers also have other platforms. For example, if an author is on the speaking circuit and always has a book table set up to sell his or her books, setting up a laptop or other electronic device that keeps repeating the book trailer will stimulate impulse purchases. Similarly, if an author can disburse one book trailer through many outlets, it will multiply the site visits. For example, the author could have the trailer available through her website, through all the websites of the writers conferences where she will be speaking in coming months, through her publisher, and also through the university where she teaches. My judgment therefore is, *use book trailers only if they are high quality and only if you can be assured they will get high visibility.*

3. **Self-Published Books.** Most writers love their manuscripts, even after they've been rejected by twenty-five publishers. That is why some will resort to paying to have their books published. In fact, as far back 2008 there were more self-published books in America than books published by traditional royalty publishers, and this trend has continued each year. But note these four points about self-published books (formerly known as "vanity" publishing): (A) most newspapers and magazines will not review self-published books; (B) most libraries will not buy or put self-published books on their shelves; (C) most bookstores will not carry self-published books; and (D) most TV and radio talk shows won't interview authors of self-published books.

So, with no publicity and no distribution, the sole responsibility of selling books falls to the author. After selling thirty-five copies to friends and family, what does the author do with the hundreds of other books stacked in the garage? List them on Amazon.com, perhaps? Well, okay, but even if orders do come in, is the author going to package each book personally, address its label, and then drive it down to the post office and stand in line?

With the right approach, self-publishing can be made to work. First, writers can try to find a sponsor to share the costs. For example, if someone is writing the history of a company, that company should help pay for the printing of the book. Second, the writer needs to establish a distribution platform. If the author has a long list of speaking engagements where he knows he can sell his books to the audiences, then, in time, he will be able to go through a thousand copies. Third, go with reliable companies that will give the names of people who have been customers of theirs. Potential customers should be told the quality of the product, the length of time until delivery, and the follow-up communication.

My judgment therefore is, *never pay for your book to be published unless you are absolutely sure you are getting a quality product and you have specific ways of selling the books.*

When asked where I feel beginning writers can spend their money most wisely, I also have suggestions. Attending a writers conference connects new writers with editors, agents, and publishers, while also providing excellent teaching sessions. Subscribing to the leading writing periodicals provides marketing updates and writing lessons. Hiring a professional critique service—wherein a well-established writer proofreads and copyedits a manuscript—can reveal writing weaknesses and sharpen one's skills. Paying dues to be part of a writers club consisting of serious writers will offer fellowship and new paths of learning.

In summary, money invested in oneself as a writer is never wasted. Money invested in so-called "shortcuts to success" has grave limitations.

## Best Publicist Tip 6
## Professional Publicity—The New "Money Pit" of Publishing

**When I was** leading workshops at the National College Media Convention in New Orleans, a university professor approached me between sessions. He said, "I got hosed royally by a publicity agent who promised to make my book a best-seller. I got taken for more than five grand, and the only thing I have to show for it is one small article in my hometown paper and a stack of printed flyers about my book. I could have done that on my own."

Sad to say, many times I've heard similar stories at writers conferences. Writers (and here I am especially talking about first-time book authors) so desire to find success in publishing, they are willing to invest thousands of dollars in publicity. They expect to wind up on the *Today Show* and *The 700 Club*, but what too often they get is an administrative assistant who is sending out waves of e-mail spam about a book no one has ever heard of or desires to hear of.

One woman told me, "My romance novel was being released by a small regional press, so I felt obligated to help promote it. The publicist I talked to in Chicago said she had lots of inside contacts with talk-show hosts, newspaper reviewers, and magazine columnists. I sent her a retainer of $3,000 and then another $3,000 two months later. I never was interviewed by anyone. I was sent a press kit that looked like something a fifth-grader had thrown together—a manila folder with three pages of a routine press release about my book, a typed review of my novel that the publicist had written, and a notice of a website where I was one of more than fifty authors squeezed into tiny boxes of news blurbs. I felt like a fool."

Many years ago when I signed a contract to coauthor a three-book mystery-romance series of novels for a Christian publisher, I got the shock of my life. I asked what the budget was for promotion and publicity, and my editor said it would be $35,000. I smiled, thinking *that should give my book a good launch.* She then said, "No, I mean the entire publicity budget for our whole company for the full year is $35,000. You are one of twenty-seven new authors who will have to share in that line item." And even worse, the money wasn't equally distributed. The company's big name authors got $5,000 apiece, leaving my coauthor and me with a couple of hundred bucks to "announce" our novels.

Not only are publicity budgets limited, so also are in-house publicists. And I mean this to now include some of the giant publishers based in New York. When Avon released my book *Millennium*

*Approaches* in mass paperback, my publicist told me that I was one of fifteen authors she was assigned to promote. Bless her heart, she got me on *Good Morning, America,* and I was featured in a large article in *USA Today*, but I've often wondered what she could have done if I'd been one of only five authors she'd been assigned to promote.

So, yes, you do have to help publicize your books. But if you decide to hire an outside agency, go into the deal with your eyes open.

Here are some guidelines:

1. **Ask for a list of clients you can contact for references.** All reputable publicists can produce such a list. Ask specific questions about what services they provided the authors, whether the publicity actually stimulated book sales, and what costs were entailed.

2. **Find a publicist who will let you be involved.** No one knows your book better than you do. As such, you could be actively involved in writing discussion questions for book clubs, providing a list of your own press contacts (hometown papers, college alumni magazines, affiliations with national organizations), and coming up with possible interview questions.

3. **Hire someone who understands your genre.** The professor who said he lost $5,000 had hired a publicist who was best known for working with romance novelists, whereas this man's book was about the life and career of the Ringling Brothers. You need someone who has a passion for what you are writing and who identifies with the readers of your genre. Indeed, it takes one to know one.

4. **Ask to see another author's press kit.** A professional press kit usually contains the author's biographical material, a summary of the book, reprints of newspaper and magazine articles written about the book or its author, a stock photo of the author, sample interview questions, and perhaps even

a printed excerpt from the book. The materials should look professional and be nicely organized.

5. **Discuss the range of media contacts and ask for verification.** Although publicists probably won't turn over to you the names and contact information of their media relations people, you can ask what venues will be contacted. If the publicist says he or she has good contacts with people at a specific talk show, ask to see a clip or to hear a recording of a client who has appeared on that show. Since most shows are now archived, that shouldn't be a problem . . . if the publicist is telling the truth.

6. **Ask about help with ancillary activities.** Some publicists can arrange for autograph parties at bookstores, teaching opportunities at writers conferences, speaking engagements at book fairs, and online webinars. These are bonus ways to promote your career and books.

With self-published and print-on-demand books now competing with traditional publishing, literally thousands of new books are being released annually. Trying to get traction for your book amidst this avalanche can be difficult. Help from a professional publicist may be appropriate, but only if you can verify a track record and have a pre-established expectation of specific areas of success. Don't waste your book's advance money on something that becomes a hasty retreat.

# Chapter 11
## Here's to Your Success

**Success Tip 1**
**Four Lessons from**
**a Bad Book**

**Someone sent me** an e-mail with the subhead, "Twenty Classic Novels You've Probably Never Read." Since I consider myself to be a well-read person, especially in literary classics, I decided to download the list and prove the sender wrong.

I was surprised to discover nine books on the list I had *not* read. That fact drove me crazy. I determined to get those books and read them pronto. But doing so proved to be one of the worst goals I've ever set.

The first book on the list was *Riders of the Purple Sage* by Zane Grey (whose real name, I swear to you, was Pearl Grey). That book should have been titled *Writer of the Purple Prose*. It's terrible—absolutely terrible.

The story is set in Utah in the Old West. Much of the book is a tirade against the Mormons and how they disrespected women, disrespected "Gentiles," and disrespected authority. At other times it becomes a pro-environmental pamphlet about preserving the animals and land of the Western territories. Yet again, it becomes a tearjerker about an orphan child whose mama died from harsh living. All of the dialogue is corny and overblown, the characters are cardboard, and the plot's resolution is depressing.

After what seemed like an eternity, I finished the book. Here's the thing that amazed me about it: I could see that every Western written (or filmed) after its publication had used this one novel as the cornerstone of what should go into a classic Western saga. I mean, in all fairness, I have to admit this novel had it all:

- Four quick-draw gunfights

- Two massive cattle stampedes

- A lone, outsider gunman with only one name: Lassiter (think *Shane* fifty years later)

- A pony that got ridden to death by its owner (think *True Grit* one hundred years later)

- A saloon brawl

- The discovery of a lost valley

- Panning for gold

- Cattle rustlers

- Ancient Indian burial grounds and cliff dwellings

- Secret hideouts behind a waterfall

- A good guy chasing bad guys on horseback

- A girl bandit

- A crooked judge

Seriously, folks, if I could do the *Reader's Digest* version of this novel and delete all the filler and editorials and melodrama, it would make an exciting story. Maybe that is why it has been made into a movie four times, each with only the highlights of the book's most exciting sections—which, as it happens, leads me to the four important lessons I learned by reading this drawn-out, boring novel.

1. **Almost all writing is improved when it is cut, reduced, edited, and tightened.** Even for fiction, the journalistic adage of "less is more" is true. Be merciless with your copy. Eliminate redundancies. Use visual nouns and thereby delete adjectives. Use action verbs and thereby delete adverbs. Make your dialogue obvious regarding who is saying the words, and thereby delete attributions. Compress scenes. Get to the point.

2. **Show, don't tell, as often as possible.** Don't spend thirty pages expounding on the need to preserve Native American culture. Have one character pick up some broken pottery and say, "This is beautiful. It should be preserved. Any way to protect these things?" Readers are bored by lectures. Action holds their attention.

3. **Give readers what they paid for.** Audiences loved Shakespeare's plays because they would get sword fights, witty dialogue, profound mysteries, political scandals, murders, ghosts, music, dancing, and heroes and villains. So, if what readers want from a Western are shoot-'em-ups and mob-scene lynchings and bank robberies and guys on white horses, then deliver the goods. Maintain momentum. Cut out the filler. On with the show!

4. **Let the good guys win.** Zane Grey's novel ends with the wealthy female landowner riding off into the sunset with the notorious gunslinger, but only after all her cattle have been taken by rustlers, her large home has been burned to the ground, her hired hands have been shot or driven off, and all but three of her horses have been stolen. What kind of justice and fair play is that? I'm all for including a touch of romance.

But please, we also need to see the varmints get what's comin' to 'em.

Now, before I get a ton of mail from irate fans of Zane Grey, let me say that yes, I know many of his novels were serialized before coming out in book form, and as such, it was accepted format back then to drag out the story for as long as possible. But Dickens managed to do that without putting readers to sleep.

As a parting thought, I will confess that I did benefit in an odd way from reading *Riders of the Purple Sage.* It taught me the four valuable lessons I've just listed.

And consequently, when I see my writer friends these days, I ask, "Hey, read any *bad* books lately?"

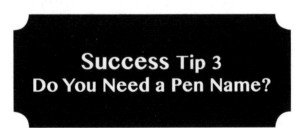

## Success Tip 3
## Do You Need a Pen Name?

**Erich Segal made** a ton of money in 1971 by churning out a little potboiler called *Love Story.* However, he was a professor of classic literature at Yale University at the time, and it was the kiss of death to his academic status. He reportedly told several friends, "I'd write that book again in a heartbeat, but never under my real name."

Evan Hunter wrote several long, involved, esteemed literary novels under his real name, but for steady cash flow, he pumped out an *87th Precinct* police procedural novel every six months for some twenty years under his popular pen name of Ed McBain.

I have written both fiction and nonfiction under a variety of pen names, including the three-book mystery-romance series for Harvest House I've mentioned before that Holly G. Miller and I co-authored under the pen name of Leslie Holden. The secret code of that name, by the way, was found by breaking down the four syllables, i.e., it was *les*s of a *lie* if we admitted we were *Hol*ly and *Den*nis.

Frequently, I'm asked at writers conferences why authors opt to use pen names. Let me explain several reasons.

1. **You may need career confidentiality.** If your primary occupation involves aspects of dealing with people in confidential matters, such as being a psychiatrist or pastor or judge or accountant, and you fear that your clientele would no longer be open to telling you personal information if folks knew you were a writer, you might opt to use a pseudonym. For example, Manfred B. Lee and Frederick Dannay, two cousins who both were attorneys for high profile clients, co-authored mystery novels under the pen name of Ellery Queen. This was kept secret for decades, until one of the cousins died.

2. **You wish to separate two or more genres.** When Holly G. Miller and I co-authored our mainstream novels, we used our real names, but when we switched genres and wrote mystery-romances, we used the pen name of Leslie Holden so that people would not confuse our two separate areas of genre writing. Similarly, that is why Evan Hunter used his real name for mainstream novels but Ed McBain for murder mysteries.

3. **Your name doesn't sound right.** No one is going to buy a combat novel called *Storming Berlin* if it is written by Lucinda Springwater. A novel like that needs to be written by someone called Sarge Murphy or Jack Gunn. It has to ring true to readers in order to be marketable. Because Western writer Zane Grey's real name was the very feminine sounding Pearl Grey, a nom de plume was called for.

4. **You are the wrong gender.** It's a known fact that men buy the majority of combat and Western novels, and they want a man's name on the cover as author. As such, when Sally E. Stuart (yes, the lady who prepared the annual *Christian Writer's Market Guide*) wrote the Western *Spirit's Gold* (Harper & Row, 1990), she wrote it under the pen name of Stuart Dillon. Conversely, women buy the vast majority of romance novels, so men who write romances use a female pen name.

   The situation used to be far worse. For many years all female writers were frowned on, so Mary Ann Evans had to write as George Eliot (*Silas Marner*, 1861). Believe it or not, Kirk Polking, who was editor of *Writer's Digest* for more than twenty years beginning in the late 1950s, was a woman. She took a man's name professionally, she told me, because when magazines were in their heyday in the post-WW II era, almost all of the freelance work went to men. (Yes, I know what her real name is, but she swore me to secrecy.)

5. **You are part of a corral of writers.** As often happens when a series of novels suddenly becomes hugely successful, numerous writers will be brought in to create individual books that showcase recurring characters in a variety of adventures. For example, all of the Hardy Boys novels carry the pen name of Franklin D. Dixon, but no such person ever existed. A dozen different ghostwriters wrote more than sixty novels in that series. The same was true for the Bobbsey Twins series and many others. (I mean, pul-ease, folks, did you honestly think that Francine Pascal actually wrote all 152 of those *Sweet Valley High* novels? Get real!)

6. **You do not wish to appear too prolific.** As an editor and feature writer for *The Saturday Evening Post*, Holly G. Miller often wrote three articles for the same issue. However, the publisher didn't want readers to think that only one person was writing the majority of the magazine, so Holly used her real name for one article, then a pen name that was a combination of her two sons' names (Charles Whitney) for a second article, and sometimes even something corny like her dog's name for

a third article (Joe Barker). Similarly, when Stephen King was pouring out novels early in his career, his publisher worried that critics and readers wouldn't believe the quality could be very good if he wrote more than one novel per year, so for several years he wrote a second novel annually but released it under the pen name of Richard Bachman (*The Running Man*, Signet, 1982).

7. **Random other reasons.** J. K. Rowling has said that she used initials for the Harry Potter novels because she felt the books would sell better if people could believe she was a man or a woman, per their preference. An Internal Revenue Service agent I know writes tax-related articles under a pen name because he feels the IRS might not be happy knowing about all the insider tips he shares with the public. A woman in the Witness Protection Program writes under a pen name because she is still in hiding. Theodore Dreiser (*An American Tragedy*, 1925) changed the spelling of his last name so as not to be confused with his brother Paul Dresser, who was a very popular composer at the time ("My Gal Sal").

One article could never contain all the reasons why writers opt to use pen names. All you need to remember is one thing: Make sure that your *real* name is on the contract and the royalty checks.

## Success Tip 2
### Beware False-Consensus Endorsements

**I was providing** fifteen-minute consultations at a large writers conference. A woman in her late thirties sat down for her appointment.[2] She put her self-published book in front of me.

On the cover was a photo of her in hair curlers and no makeup. She was shown holding a frying pan in one hand and balancing a baby on her hip with the other hand. The book's title in garish purple letters was *Life in the Fast Pain: How to Be a Go-Go Gal in a Gone-Gone Body.* The byline read, *by Bonnie "the zany mom" Davis.*

On the back cover were cutesy endorsements, including, "Now that *she's* a mom, Bonnie knows why she drove me nuts," from Mrs. Cynthia Becker, identified as "Bonnie's Mom" (thanks for explaining that one); and "I knew even in third grade when Bonnie would stand on her head in front of the class, she was destined to become a comic one day," from Mrs. MacIntosh, identified as (can you see it coming?) "Bonnie's third-grade teacher."

I stared at the woman. I was amazed at how she looked nothing like her persona on the cover. Instead, she had on a smartly styled pantsuit, snazzy patent leather shoes, and classy contemporary jewelry, all set off by a modern frosted hairstyle.

I asked her how I could help her, pretty much knowing what she was about to say.

---

2. The incident is real, but the name of the writer and the title of the book have been changed.

"People have always told me I'm funny," she began. "I'm the life of the party everywhere I go. So, three years ago I started speaking at mother-daughter banquets, PTA meetings, and Girl Scout retreats. I never charged anything because I was just getting started. My goal, however, was to become another Erma Bombeck, traveling around the country, giving talks at conventions, conferences, and women's gatherings. Make some TV appearances, too."

"Erma's been dead for more than a decade," I pointed out.

"All the more reason for someone new to come along," she countered, totally undeterred. "Anyway, I wrote up all my funny stories, but no one would publish my book because I didn't have a national platform yet. So, my husband and I borrowed $7,000, and we self-published this book. Now, I have a garage filled with unsold books; and, unfortunately for me, requests for personal appearances are *not* pouring in. So, where'd I go wrong? I mean, I *know* I'm funny. *Everyone* says so."

This woman was a victim of what is known as "false consensus syndrome." For example, people will say, "Let's eat at that café. Look at all the trucks parked outside." To that, I'd be one to ask, "And who, may I inquire, ever said a trucker was any kind of judge of what qualifies as gourmet food?"

Here was the problem with Bonnie, the unsuccessful comic. She liked to tell jokes. People would always give a courtesy laugh, even if they thought her jokes were lame. Also, she liked to speak in front of groups. The groups would give her a round of applause, mostly because the folks listening were thinking, *Better her than me,* since most people hate public speaking.

Furthermore, she gave her typed book manuscript to her mom, husband, best friends, sister, and neighbors and she asked for "honest feedback." Because these folks loved her, they refused to be cruel. So they responded with what they imagined she wanted to hear: "It sounds just like you." "It's really amusing." "I enjoyed it." "Thanks for sharing this with me. It was quite entertaining."

And so, with these "enthusiastic" endorsements, Bonnie concluded she was ready for the big time. She wasn't, of course. Nevertheless, she spent borrowed money to print her book and then found herself in the wilderness of would-be comics and would-be authors. It proved to be a very, *very* lonely place.

When it comes to test marketing, authors like Bonnie should be no less diligent than companies. Manufacturers constantly reevaluate their developing products. They want to make sure, before they invest a large amount of start-up capital, that the end product will be something the public will buy. Writers should follow similar procedures. Here's how to go about it.

1. **Get feedback from experts, not friends and relatives.** Certain people hire me to edit their manuscripts. My rates are rather steep, but after these folks have gotten rejected a dozen or more times, they're ready to find out why they can't sell their books. Folks in their writers club have praised them for their creativity. I don't praise them. Instead, I grab a red pen and start slashing.

   I point out errors in spelling, grammar, punctuation, format, style, syntax, transitions, logic, and continuity. I help them identify stilted dialogue, ambiguous descriptions, vague characterizations, unrealistic coincidences, vapid plotting concepts, and tedious backstory summaries.

   For novice writers, this editing can be painful, often brutally so. However, it can also be revealing. At least now these people know exactly what is wrong and precisely how to go about fixing it. Their friends weren't—and often didn't know *how* to be—so forthright. It required an outside expert who had qualifications and bluntness and professionalism. Take this lesson to heart for yourself: Make the effort to find an expert.

2. **Make sure you hear what is being said.** In Bonnie's case, people told her she was fun to be around, but (being desperate for approval) Bonnie heard that as, "You're as funny

as a professional comedienne." People gave her polite applause, but she interpreted that as a rousing cheer.

She didn't listen to what was actually being said; she heard only what she wanted to hear. That's self-deception. In the end, Bonnie became her own worst enemy. But you can learn from her mistake. If you ask for feedback, don't talk. Just listen intently, accept the praise or criticism, and then adjust your public speaking or professional writing accordingly.

3. **Acquire endorsements that have credibility.** Bonnie thought that including quotes from her mom and her elementary teacher would be a cute idea for her book cover. The result was neither funny nor credible. I'm sure Suzanne Collins and James Patterson could have gotten endorsements from their mothers too, but why should they have bothered? For my latest book on aspects of professional writing, I obtained endorsements from two magazine editors, a college writing professor, and three best-selling authors. Now that's clout.

If Bonnie had approached some professional speakers or comics for endorsements, one of two things would have happened: They would have turned her down, and Bonnie would have discovered her book really wasn't funny enough to be published. Or they would have given her the endorsements, and that would have greatly helped her sell the books. Credible endorsements *are* factors that convince people to buy a book. So, seek the right folks.

4. **Do your own test marketing.** Before you become a literary lemming and run off a cliff, go only partway down that path.

Bonnie should have tested her skills in smaller venues before instantly trying for the big time. She should have written some comedic articles about life as a housewife, mom, or Tupperware party-planner.

She could have sent them to a national magazine or even to her local newspaper. If they were accepted and published, and if she got letters from readers along with invitations to speak, this would have been verification of her talent.

Conversely, if Bonnie's writings all came back rejected, this would have made her bluntly aware that her style and delivery, and perhaps even content, needed more work. Likewise, if word-of-mouth advertising generated a lot more calls for her to speak after she did her small-venue talks to the PTA and scouting groups, that would have been evidence she had a winning presentation. If no calls came, however, she would realize the need to refine her content and delivery.

We all crave praise and compliments. We harbor dreams of fame and success. But if these fantasies blind us to the realities of our levels of talent or preparation, the results will be emotionally devastating and financially crippling. We have to let other people hold a mirror before us and describe what the real reflection is, not what we wish it would be.

Those writers who are bold enough to face reality are usually also bold enough to perform whatever surgery is required to shape the image into what is required to fulfill the fantasy—a better-written manuscript, a stronger national platform, and more polishing of one's professional skills.

Don't be swayed by a false consensus of your talents. Deal with reality.

## Success Tip 4
## The Music of Writing:
## Maestro or Second Fiddle?

**I worked my** way through college by playing in a five-piece combo and teaching guitar lessons at a music store. I was good enough to think about making music my career, but an incident during my teen years caused me to change my mind.

My brother and I had written some country music songs. We went to a small studio in Michigan and cut six demos. We drove to Nashville and started making the rounds of the major recording companies to pitch our songs. We didn't rack up any sales that trip (years later I'd have better luck in selling some gospel tunes I wrote), but we had a chance to listen in on some recording sessions.

I was stunned by the talent of the amazing session musicians. Yet they weren't stars in their own right. They just sat by the phone each day and hoped their union rep would call and say they were needed for a session. On a very, very, *very* rare occasion, one of these "sidemen" would emerge as a solo act, such as happened to Jerry Reed, Glen Campbell, James Burton, and Barbara Mandrell. But for each breakout artist, there were seven hundred master musicians who continued to work for scale and remained anonymous.

### Singin' the Blues

Curious about this, I questioned some of the sidemen about what it took to break out. This is what they told me.

One woman, a pianist, said, "I'm one of the best sight-readers anywhere. Put a sheet of music in front of me, and I can play it to perfection within minutes. But that's all I do. I play other people's music. I've never composed anything original. I'm a reader, not a writer."

A guitarist, mid-twenties, told me, "I've hung around country pickers all my life—barn dances, honkytonks, jamborees. I know every lick and chord from Hank Williams to Buck Owens. Trouble is, that's the extent of my range. I don't play jazz riffs. I've never mastered flamenco finger-style playing. I couldn't play a classical number to save my life. I'm the best at what I do, but what I do is just one slice of the musical pie. As a result, I miss out on a lot of work."

An older fellow who played standing bass told me, "I've always made a basic living by being flexible and content. If someone needed a bass player and background singer for a three-month road tour, I'd sign on. If a local radio station needed a bass player for a Sunday morning gospel hour, I'd take the job. I'd do session work, fill in at bars…whatever was available. Trouble was, I never became a specialist at anything. I never developed a unique style, an original sound. I was content to earn a paycheck by being 'good enough.' I was adequate, not distinctive."

## They're Playin' Your Swan Song

Today, after many years of teaching at numerous writers conferences from coast to coast, I have seen parallels between talented musicians and talented writers. The writing world has lots and lots of sidemen, too—reporters for modest-circulation newspapers, poets who've been published only in obscure literary quarterlies, playwrights whose works have never made it past the church or school stage, English teachers who are still working on that novel started back in college.

They all fantasize about hitting the *New York Times* best-seller list, winning the Pulitzer Prize, getting a screen-adaptation offer from Spielberg, and being profiled in *The New Yorker*. So…why ain't it happenin'? For identical reasons as the musicians, actually.

Like the piano player, many would-be writers spend their primetime hours reading other people's works rather than creating their own. Reading is critical to the development of a writer; but *writers must write*. Striving for a balance is crucial.

Like the guitarist, many new writers limit their development by exploring only one genre *ad infinitum*. The pros don't do that. Jerry B. Jenkins writes mysteries, police procedurals, end-times novels, and biographies. Joyce Carol Oates writes essays, reviews, novels, short stories, and literary criticism. Liz Curtis Higgs writes magazine comedy columns, historical novels, and nonfiction books about biblical characters and themes. The wider a writer's range of talents, the greater the amount of work he or she will generate. Thus, amplify your talents, amplify your success.

Like the bass player, too many fledgling writers waste time dabbling rather than focusing. Sure, when we're novices, we're willing to accept any writing assignment offered to us. That's survival. However, it's not progress. To advance, a writer needs to master a skill-set, gain a reputation and following, and then move to other levels of expertise, always securing a readership based on genuine talent. I began as a journalist myself, then started selling freelance magazine articles, became a columnist, wrote nonfiction books, then novels, then textbooks, and recently a stage play.

Sidemen…well…sit on the sides. They supplement the stars. The stars stand out. They are the soloists. Writers have the same options: sit on the sidelines or rise to star status. It's a decision and a process.

What about you: maestro or second fiddle?

## Success Tip 5
## The Power of
## Negative Thinking

**Those of you** who have followed my career for the past several decades may be surprised that I'm writing about the value of negative thinking. Yes, yes, I know, I'm the guy who wrote the 1982 best-seller *Positive Workaholism*, and my book *The Power of Positive Productivity* has been translated globally into five foreign languages—including Romanian—since 2005.

What I want to talk about, however, is not a glum, hopeless, defeatist negativity. Instead, it is a cautionary, pragmatic, logical form of negativity. In short, it is a system of analysis that can help a writer be prepared for any negative situation that could possibly arise, and, thus, take proactive steps to avoid potential disaster.

### Anticipating a Worst-Case Scenario

Let's use a real-life situation. Imagine you are going to a writers conference and you are scheduled to meet for fifteen minutes with an acquisitions editor. You intend to introduce yourself, talk about your book, and, with luck, leave your book proposal with that editor. Okay, prior to the conference, start asking yourself, "What might possibly go awry in this meeting to ruin my chances of making a good first impression?"

Be harsh. Be real. Be honest. Make a list.

1. **My appearance might be negative in some way.** Remember to press your clothes, get a haircut, clean your nails, use a breath mint, and tone down the cologne.
2. **My book proposal may not be complete.** Double-check to make sure you have a cover letter, cover page, synopsis, table of contents, author biography, outline, and three sample

chapters. Bring a spare proposal in case the first editor you talk to asks to keep your only copy. Bring a flash drive containing the entire book proposal in case you need to print even more copies or e-mail it as an attachment.

3. **The editor may ask me questions I don't know how to answer.** Find someone in your writers club or critique group who has done this before, and have that person provide possible questions you'll need answers for. Ask that person to sit and do a mock run-through with you so you can rehearse your pitch.

## Running a different scenario

Let's say that you want to leave your salaried job and turn to freelance writing as a full-time occupation. Make a detailed list of everything that could possibly go wrong.

1. **I might not be able to pay my monthly bills.** Line up some steady writing jobs in advance, such as writing a church or company newsletter, doing weekend columns for your local newspaper, or teaching a writing class at a community college.

2. **What if I get sick or injured and cannot write for a few weeks?** Make sure all of your insurance plans are in place before resigning your job.

3. **What if my published book is a flop?** Don't enter full-time writing based on the publication of one book. Have a body of work earning royalties for you before you pull the plug on your regular income.

4. **What if my family doesn't respect my need for privacy?** Set up a home office, declare your workday schedule, explain to the family that this is how you'll make it possible for them to eat, and then enforce your work regimen.

## Learning from Negative Experiences

In spite of excellent preplanning, things can still go amiss. If so, benefit from that. For example, after a poor interview with an acquisitions editor, make some notes (literally, on paper or using a mobile device). Remind yourself, *Have business cards next time. Leave early for the appointment in case of a traffic jam on the way. Bring some information on people who can endorse my book. Don't forget to have something printed out about my personal platform and my publicity ideas for helping to sell my book, once published.*

This is called course correction. Sure, you may have crashed on the rocks in this first interview by not being adequately prepared, but next time you'll steer clear of hazardous waters. Forewarned is forearmed. Don't make the same mistakes twice.

If the world of publishing has learned anything during the past decade, it is this lesson: Those who avoid facing the potential negative aspects of situations are doomed to failure. Publishers at the beginning of the twenty-first century should have been asking such negative questions as, "What if these e-books aren't just a passing fad? What if online publishing actually starts to grow more rapidly than traditional publishing? What if self-publishing becomes inexpensive and competitive?"

Burying your head in the sand is no way to change the inevitable. Better to anticipate problems and changes so you can embrace solutions and answers.

## Everyone Is Impacted

I sit on the board of directors of two large writers conferences, one for the Christian market, one for the general market. I have made very positive changes in our class offerings, our selection of faculty, even our venue for holding the conferences, by constantly bringing up negative scenarios.

For example, a few years ago I said, "What if younger writers don't like keynote addresses and workshops done by lecturing?" As a result, one conference initiated interactive learning with students sitting at keyboards, instructors using smart boards (interactive white boards), and all work being done paperless. The enrollment at that conference for the age group of thirty and younger has tripled during the past couple of years.

Again let me stress that I am not a defeatist, only a pragmatist. Life hasn't always worked out well for me. I was injured in Vietnam. My daughter was born with a complete heart block. A spring flood inundated the entire lower floor of one of my rental properties. Some of my books have gotten lousy reviews.

Hey, life is tough, and you can't always see what is coming at you from your blindside. As such, like Joseph in Egypt, you lay up seven years of grain in anticipation of seven years of famine. It's good to have a plan B and also a plan C. Anticipate what could go wrong and try to prevent it. If it goes wrong anyway, learn from that and be better next time.

I'm positive this will work for you.

**Most of the** writers I know—at least if they're honest—will confess to having a major project they would love to "find the time" to write. It might be a screenplay, stage drama, musical, novel, or (in my case) a serious work of literary criticism. The intention is to write this masterpiece sometime before dying, yet the months and years keep zipping by with little or no progress on it.

It makes me wonder. I mean, if it's so important, why isn't *anything* being done about writing it?

In reality, the answer is obvious. It's also logical, pragmatic... and sad.

Some writers don't tackle the big project due to fear. They worry they might invest huge amounts of valuable time only to find out that it wasn't such a great idea or, far worse, it *was* a great idea, but they didn't have the talent to bring it off.

Other writers have the confidence that they could complete the project, but they wonder if in the long run it might fail to equate *financially* to the lesser projects they are now involved in.

Still others have such high regard for the project, they feel they would not do it justice unless they had long stretches of undivided time to give to it. And, since such a breadth of open time has not presented itself, by necessity the project has to wait—until retirement? until the kids are out of college? until the family can live on one income?

## The Twenty-Five-Year Pregnancy

I know all about this postponement game. I left my salaried job in 1982 and turned to freelance writing full time. With a wife and two kids to support, I had to hustle. I wrote columns, interviews, comedy sketches, devotions, reviews, mystery stories, romance novels, and songs. My wife and kids never missed any meals, and I racked up a lot of bylines and thoroughly enjoyed what I was doing. I've always stayed busy. In fact, with all the published books, articles, and short stories to my credit, probably more than one hack would gladly trade places with me. It's been a good run so far.

But there's the academic side to me too. Ever since completing my PhD in English, I've carried a desire to contribute something to the world of literary criticism. My dream was to prepare a fully documented, completely annotated edition of Jack London's classic novel *Martin Eden* one day.

*Martin Eden* was the book that had long ago convinced me I wanted to spend my life as a writer, and it also led me to doing my doctoral dissertation on the life and writings of Jack London. The problem was, one didn't just sit down and knock out something like that. So, I said, "Yeah, one day I'll get to it. One day, for sure."

I found that I enjoyed teaching the literary elements of that novel at writers conferences and when I was a guest professor at various colleges. I'd also occasionally reread sections of it and make marginal notes to myself about scenes, characters, dialogue, foreshadowing, flashbacks, and historical elements. However, to annotate it exhaustively would have taken many months. And I felt I didn't have that amount of time to devote to something that would not be financially rewarding, even if I could find a publisher. So, I carried that baby for a quarter of a century, dreaming of its birth but never taking it to the delivery room.

Then one day life stopped. I walked out of a building on March 1, 2004, stepped into a mud puddle during a rainstorm, slipped, fell, and cracked my left pelvic socket. Instantly, I was disabled. The physicians told me I'd be as good as new...in about five months. Meanwhile, I'd be bedridden for three weeks, in a wheelchair for two months, on crutches for another month, and then on a cane for several additional weeks.

*Were they kidding?* Man, I'd fought in Vietnam for twelve months and had never broken a bone or sustained a serious wound. And now—what?—a guy with six combat medals was flattened by a mud puddle? The irony, the outrageousness, the incredibility of it all exceeded my ability to express my utter frustration. I actually screamed.

## I Wasn't Irreplaceable

So, a slip in the mud put me out of commission for five months. At the time I was a full-time college professor in the middle of the spring semester. To my amazement, the dean actually found someone to come in and sub for me for three weeks until I could get to campus in a wheelchair. *I had an equal?*

Just as humbling, my editors said they could use my "evergreen" columns on file to buy me a few months off and then they could use "guest columnists" on a rotation until I was well enough to write again. *My loyal readers wouldn't rise up in revolt?*

Yikes! What does one do when one is laid flat on his back 24/7 and is not needed by the world?

Well, for me, one option was, *write a masterpiece.*

All I could do was prop myself on a pillow and hold a book at my chest. Okay, I made that book *Martin Eden.* I flipped on a tape recorder and started dictating notes about each scene, each chapter, each character. I asked my wife to bring me my files. I propped them one at a time on my chest, and I dictated notes from them, too. As the tapes filled, I had them transcribed. I then propped the transcriptions on my chest, and I read into the tape recorder what editing changes were needed.

The crazy thing was, despite the constant pain from my cracked bone, I couldn't remember being that happy in years. My life's dream was finally becoming a reality.

Yes, I eventually walked again. And, yes, I finished the annotated edition of *Martin Eden* and had three university presses vie for publishing rights. It went through only one print run of one thousand copies, and the majority of them wound up being purchased by libraries, but the book was 603 pages and beautiful and was hailed by literary journals as "the definitive scholarly analysis of Jack London's autobiographical novel." I knew then, I could die a contented soul (although I plan to put that off for a few decades). Even now, as I glance across my office to the shelves and see that book's two-inch spine and my name and Jack's there together, I nod and smile. *Write on, Bro'.*

The story of how I finally wrote my dream book contains a lesson for other writers. Several lessons, actually.

1. **Writing your masterpiece is never really about the money.** It's about self-fulfillment. So, if you steal time away from other "filler" jobs in order to write your dream project and it never ends up making you a fortune (maybe never even gets published, heaven forbid), you'll still know you had the moxie to create it. You'll sleep with a smile on your face. You won't spend the rest of your days wondering, "What if…?" All in all, that's pretty valuable. (And, geez, it might *become* a best-seller.)

2. **You might be surprised by what new career options your masterpiece may open for you.** Shortly after my annotated edition of *Martin Eden* started getting reviewed in literary quarterlies, I was invited to lecture about Jack London at Oxford University. I accepted. My wife went along. She also went along when several similar invitations came my way. Traveling around the world on someone else's nickel can be fun.

3. **You'll realize sooner or later that it all comes down to priorities.** Yes, there is enough time to write your masterpiece. The world won't grind to a halt if you go on sabbatical, or if you step off three committees for a year, or if

you give up the bowling and golf leagues for two seasons. I pray it won't take a crippling accident to teach you *that* lesson!

4. **You need to realize now that when they prepare to write your obituary, they won't be listing small stuff.** Your gardening column in the *Villeville Gazette* and your cover story for that financial investment magazine won't be blips on anyone's radar screen. However, your one big project—oh, yeah, *that one*—will prove to the world that it was good you were born.

So, contribute. Leave something substantial behind. Write your masterpiece.

# About the Authors

## Dennis E. Hensley

Dennis E. Hensley, PhD, is Professor of Communication (Professional Writing concentration) in the Communication Department at Taylor University in Upland, Indiana. He is the author of more than 60 books, including eight textbooks on aspects of professional writing, as well as stage plays, musicals, film scripts, and 3,500 newspaper and magazine articles.

Dr. Hensley has received the Award for Teaching Excellence from Indiana University (1990), the Dorothy Hamilton Memorial Writing Award from Ball State University (1993), the City of Fort Wayne Bicentennial Gold Medallion (1996), and the Elizabeth Sherrill Lifetime Achievement Award (2009). He served as the Distinguished Visiting Scholar in English and Journalism at the Graduate School of Communication Arts at Regent University (2001–02), Distinguished Visiting Lecturer at Oxford University (2006), Distinguished Visiting Literary Scholar at Moody Bible Institute (2007), and Distinguished Visiting Professor of American Literature at York St. John University in England (2014). He has also received distinguished alumnus awards from T. L. Handy High School, Delta College, and Saginaw Valley State University. During 1970 and 1971, Dr. Hensley served as a sergeant in the United States Army and was awarded six medals for service in Vietnam.

Currently, Dr. Hensley sits on the Board of Directors of the Midwest Writers Workshop (Indiana). He is an annual judge for all three of the major Christian writing competitions: the Gold Medallion/Christian Book Awards, the Christy Fiction Awards, and the Evangelical Press Association Awards. He is a columnist for *Christian Communicator* and a popular speaker at writers conferences worldwide. Learn more at www.dochensley.com.

## Diana Savage

Diana Savage has written or contributed to 12 books, including two Chicken Soup for the Soul volumes, and has published more than 200 articles, short stories, and poems. She speaks at a variety of venues in the US and abroad and directs the annual Northwest Christian Writers Renewal conference near Seattle.

As the principal at Savage Creative Services, LLC, she provides professional writing, editing, and speaking services. She earned her BA degree from Northwest University and her Master in Theological Studies degree from Bakke Graduate University. She has served on the board of directors of four nonprofits, as director of women's ministries at a large West Coast church, and as development officer for a ministry to homeless children and their families. Learn more at www.dianasavage.com.

# Additional Book by
# Doc Hensley

## from
## Bold Vision Books

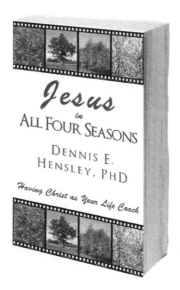

If you desire to excel in personal goal achievement and want to find how to live a successful Christian life, *Jesus in All Four Seasons* will help you observe Jesus as a life coach for every situation. This entertaining "fact-vella" (a factual book with a novella inserted within it) provides a powerful message for business, industry, and management, goal setting, inspiration, and creative thinking.

An Imprint of Bold Vision Books

Check out these books on the craft of
writing, speaking, acting, and business.

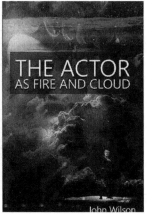

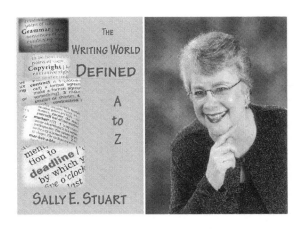

www.boldvisionbooks.com

Made in the USA
Lexington, KY
23 May 2017